Norfolk

COUNTRYSIDE BOOKS
NEWBURY BERKSHIRE

First published 2004

COUNTRYSIDE BOOKS
3 Catherine Road
Newbury, Berks

To view our complete range of books,
please visit us at
www.countrysidebooks.co.uk

ISBN 1 85306 878 0

Designed by Peter Davies, Nautilus Design
Produced through MRM Associates Ltd., Reading
Printed by Woolnough Bookbinding Ltd., Irthlingborough

CONTENTS

CONTENTS

Introduction

Selecting outstanding characters for a volume like this is a humbling experience no matter how familiar you might be with some of their exceptional exploits. Simply moving among those 'admired for great deeds and noble qualities' – possibly the best short summary of what constitutes a hero or heroine – brings on a deep mood of personal inadequacy. Thankfully, that can give way to a fresh surge of ambition as inspiring figures from across the Norfolk centuries line up to take well-deserved bows.

They are figures of substance and real achievement, especially when placed alongside the inflated egos and blank cheques swirling around today's transient worlds of sport and entertainment. Too many passing shadows are elevated to instant heroic status on the back of a winning goal in injury time, or an outrageous contribution to our celebrity-infested television schedules.

Of course, I could have extended my roll of honour by dozens without resorting to the margins of fame and fortune, but to those who complain about certain omissions let me suggest a new twist to an old maxim: 'There, but for the grace of publishers, go I!' Choices, unfortunately, had to be made.

A number of Norfolk legends picked themselves – Henry Blogg, Edith Cavell, George Edwards and Horatio Nelson for a start – but I was determined to include a few sadly-neglected achievers, most notably in the field of women's writing, among them Fanny Burney, Mary Mann, Harriet Martineau and Doreen Wallace. It is perhaps an opportune time also for diminutive Sarah Martin to step away from the shadow of Elizabeth Fry in the sphere of prison reform, and for teachers Tom and Kitty Higdon to collect overdue marks for inspiring the longest strike in English history.

My sporting interests urged forward Jem Mace, father of modern boxing, heavyweight champion of the world and lucky enough to be born in the same village as me. Then there was cricketer Bill Edrich, whose courage as a wartime flyer was matched by an unquenchable spirit of cavalier defiance at the crease. He came home to Norfolk after a glittering first-class career to inspire the old county to new heights.

Perhaps a couple of selections may be placed in the 'controversial' bracket, although my admiration remains unshaken by strains of eccentricity in vastly different arenas. Lucilla Reeve took on a derelict farm and the full might of the military authorities when Breckland villages were turned into a battleground. Allan Smethurst also ploughed a highly individual furrow as the Singing Postman, taking his brand of Norfolk culture into forbidden territory despite personal frailties destined to cut short that colourful journey.

I am grateful to countless scribes for producing books, pamphlets and articles to enlighten us generally over the years, and to good friends for providing valuable help in researching and illustrating the following pages. Special salutes here to Ann English, Carol Twinch and Steve Snelling.

My wife Diane displayed her customary relish for greatly valued supporting roles both in the study and on the road. These results underline the true value of combining old-fashioned enthusiasm with modern technology. No heroics from me in connection with the latter!

Keith Skipper

1

Bill Edrich (1916–1986)

A Cricketing Legend

My Coronation Year scrapbook for 1953 is packed with sporting heroes alongside the first conquerors of Mount Everest. There's the veteran winger Stanley Matthews inspiring Blackpool to a pulsating 4-3 win over Bolton in one of Wembley's most memorable FA Cup Finals. There's Gordon Richards landing his first Derby in 28 attempts aboard *Pinza*. There's dashing Denis Compton hitting the winning runs at the Oval as England take back the Ashes from the Aussies for the first time in two decades. But it was the chap batting at the other end who crowned that wonderful sporting year for me; a home-grown hero from Norfolk's most famous cricketing clan.

Bill Edrich, probably the finest sportsman the county has produced, conquered fast-bowling, late-night parties and beautiful women. He was a brilliant back-foot batsman, a superb hooker and player of offspin, and his courage was legendary even in a sporting age when courage and chivalry were unremarkable.

Bill was born on March 26, 1916 at Lingwood, eight miles east of Norwich, into an old established Norfolk family of farmers already known for their cricketing prowess. Three of Bill's brothers also played the first-class game, Eric and Geoffrey for Lancashire, and Brian for Kent and Glamorgan. Cousin John made his big mark for Surrey and England. Over the years teams made up entirely of the Edrich family played many popular fixtures.

As a 16 year old pupil at Bracondale School in Norwich in

Bill Edrich

1932, Bill went out to face the All-India tourists at Lakenham with Norfolk floundering on 21 for 5. He made 20 in 40 minutes. For the first time, Edrich defiance was written into the records.

Although 2,000 runs in each of three pre-war seasons confirmed his outstanding abilities, there were lingering doubts about his Test match temperament. A nightmare baptism against the Australians in 1938 – just 67 runs in six innings – continued in South Africa the following year with 21 runs in five innings. But England captain Wally Hammond kept faith in the young man from Norfolk, and in the 'timeless' fifth Test Edrich piled up 240 runs.

That unquenchable spirit on the field was soon to be put to the test in the wartime arena. Bill, as a Pilot Officer in the celebrated 107 Squadron based at Great Massingham, took his Blenheim on several horrendously dangerous operations over Germany, including the first daylight raid on the Ruhr. 'Billy, boy, we'd follow you anywhere,' said one Canadian flier. Edrich won the Distinguished Flying Cross and led other hazardous attacks on heavily-fortified German installations. These death-defying operations were to have a profound effect on his future life, every day coming as a bonus to be enjoyed.

One raid was mounted only hours before Bill's squadron were due to play a cricket match against a Massingham XI. Edrich flew through a storm of fire and made it back safely, but two crews did not. Their places were taken by substitutes and the match went ahead, though the memory of so much death and destruction was never far away. Poignantly recalling that cricket encounter, Edrich wrote: 'Every now and then would come the old accustomed cry ... OWZATT! – and then one's mind would flicker off to the briefing and to joking with a pal whose broken body was now washing in the long, cold tides, and one saw again his machine cartwheeling down, flaming from nose to tail, and then a ball would roll fast along the green English turf and in the distance the village clock would strike and the mellow echoes would ring through the lazy air of that perfect summer afternoon.'

So the slaughter continued. During one particularly audacious raid on power stations in Cologne, the squadron again suffered severely. Edrich, who always wore his England sweater beneath his flying jacket, came through unscathed then as by some miracle he would continue to do, until he was taken off operations and given a staff job.

After the war Bill's devil-may-care lifestyle enlivened the austerity gloom, above all in partnership with his Middlesex 'twin' Denis Compton during that rhapsodic, record-breaking summer of 1947, when Bill scored 3,539 runs and Compton 3,816. Bill's high spirits upset some in authority, however, and he was dropped from the 1951 tour of Australia. Restored to favour, he played a major part in winning back the Ashes in Coronation Year.

During 1952, in fading light at Lord's he was felled by a bouncer from Frank 'Typhoon' Tyson, reckoned by no less an authority than Sir Donald Bradman to be the fastest bowler he had ever seen. Edrich's cheekbone was fractured, but to the astonishment of all he returned to the wicket next morning, his jaw in a sling, his eyes almost closed by massive facial bruising. Tyson's first ball was another bouncer. 'Believe it or not, Bill tried to hook it,' recalled Frank. 'You simply could not intimidate him.'

After retirement from first-class cricket in 1958, he returned to his native county and led Norfolk for eleven seasons. 'Seldom can the enjoyment of the players have been better communicated to spectators, seldom can a side have had a better team spirit,' said former Norfolk secretary David Armstrong. When he played for Norfolk between 1932 and 1936, Edrich scored 2,160 runs and took 119 wickets. By the end of his second spell with the county, these figures stood at 8,308 and 417 respectively.

Bill was also a talented soccer player. He had made his football league debut for Spurs against Blackpool in 1935 but was forced out of the game six years later by strained knee ligaments.

He married no less than five times – 'Bill was always falling in love,' said his old friend Trevor Bailey. Former Middlesex colleague John Warr, asked to attend one of Bill's weddings, recalled being told he needed an invitation to get in. 'Invitation?' he queried, 'I've got a season ticket for Bill's weddings!' Alan Hill, Edrich's biographer, said his character juxtaposed honourable and wanton elements. Caring, kind and never deliberately hurtful, he notes, beyond the heartbreaks of the estrangements was the remarkable legacy of lingering affection. 'The tender forgiveness of Bill's ladies in retirement is a testimony to an infuriating but disarming man.'

Ian Wooldridge wrote: 'Bill Edrich epitomised the peculiarly British breed of incurable scallywag. He loved life too much to harbour grudges, sustain feuds or niggle opponents, with whom, like as not, he'd be out on the tiles at the close of play. But there was a bottom line to the roistering. You had to be there before the start of play next day. Then, hungover or otherwise, you had to fight.'

Five years after his death a stand at his beloved Lord's was named after him and dedicated to his memory – next to one similarly dedicated to Denis Compton. Sentinels of a remembrance of a glorious era when a Norfolk farmer's boy went to cricket headquarters to reap such a rich harvest.

Bill Edrich fought for England on the hallowed turf and in the war-torn skies. He led my parade of Coronation Year sporting heroes . . . and came home to Norfolk for a glorious Indian summer.

2

Henry Blogg (1876–1954)

Cromer's Famous Lifeboatman

Hailed as the greatest lifeboatman this country has ever known, Cromer's Henry Blogg was the man everybody had heard of – and nobody really knew. Solitary and shy, he was lionised as the archetypal silent hero. The less he said, the more the publicity machines made of him.

Bare statistics can merely hint at the qualities and achievements of a born leader. Coxswain of the Cromer boat for 38 years, he gave 53 years of service in all. During that time the Cromer boats were out 387 times and saved 873 lives. He retired in 1947 at the age of 71. No other lifeboatman has won as many medals as Henry Blogg. He was awarded the gold medal (the lifeboatman's VC) three times and the silver medal four times. He also won the George Cross and the British Empire Medal.

It is a measure of his fame that 'Blogg of Cromer' was as instantly recognisable as such sporting heroes as Len Hutton of Yorkshire and England and Sir Malcolm Campbell and *Bluebird*. In this unassuming, non-swimming Norfolk fisherman, who rarely ventured out of his home patch, the Royal National Lifeboat Institution found a most unlikely *beau ideal*. He was the epitome of the ordinary rendered extraordinary. But, try as they might, very few have been able to get anywhere near to unravelling the hidden depths behind one of the country's greatest seafarers, a man whose understanding of the hazardous waters and changing sandbanks off the Norfolk coast was second to none.

HENRY BLOGG (1876–1954)

Henry Blogg, the lifeboat legend

Henry lived all his 78 years in Cromer. He was born on 6th February, 1876 in a cottage in New Street – now the Wellington Inn – opposite the pier and almost in the shadow of the magnificent parish church. As a youngster he spent several years in the care of Granny Blogg in Garden Street before moving to the home of his stepfather John James Davies, in Chapel Street. Henry went to the Goldsmith's School on the corner of Overstrand Road. It had originally been founded as a free grammar school in 1505 by Sir Bartholomew Bede, a native of Cromer who became a Lord Mayor of London.

One who knew him better than most was Henry 'Shrimp' Davies, his nephew and fishing partner who went on to succeed this formidable figure as a Cromer coxswain of outstanding distinction in his own right. 'Shrimp' died in 2002 at the age of 88. 'His greatest strength was his willpower. I don't think he ever broke a promise in his life, either to himself or anybody else,' said the proud nephew. 'He stopped smoking at 16 when he saw himself in the mirror with a cigarette dangling out of his mouth and thought "Henry Blogg, you look like a pig with a straw in its mouth!" so he threw the fag on the fire and the packet with it.

'Then there was the time he decided to give up alcohol. He'd got drunk at 18, and the next morning he told my grandfather he'd never touch another drop. And he didn't. You couldn't force it down him, not even when they pulled him out of the water when he got washed overboard during the *English Trader* rescue. They couldn't give him a drop of rum.

'But the thing I admire about him most of all is the way he just decided to stop swearing. After his only daughter died, he never came out of doors for almost a fortnight after the funeral. And when he did, he never swore again. I can understand a man giving up smoking or drinking, but how do you change your natural way of talking?' asked 'Shrimp' with a rueful smile. This was the brand of determination wedded to self-belief and supreme seamanship that characterised all of Blogg's lifeboat service.

To select just one chapter from this adventure-packed saga of the seas: it was a dramatic mission on 9th January 1917 that signalled the birth of a lifeboat legend. The rescue of eleven crewmen from the shattered hulk of the Swedish ship the SS *Fernebo* represented one of the bravest and most spectacular services ever undertaken by lifeboatmen around our shores. Despite having already carried out one launch that same day, Blogg and his indomitable crew, with an average age of over 50

– the war had drawn away the younger men to the Navy and merchant fleet – succeeded at the third attempt in battling through a north-easterly gale to reach the stricken wreck, some 400 yards off shore. It was an astonishing feat of seamanship and cold-blooded courage, made all the more remarkable by the fact it was performed in an open boat powered only by oars and the raw strength of the crew.

By the time they pulled alongside the front section of the *Fernebo*, guided by an anti-aircraft searchlight, they had been combating the elements for nearly 14 gruelling hours. Commander Basil Hall, Inspector of Lifeboats, watched the rescue in awe. He later wrote: 'Bathed in the brilliant beam of the searchlight, one moment standing on end as she mounted the crest of a huge breaker, at another with her nose buried in the trough of the sea, or completely lost to sight as a sea broke right over her, the lifeboat made a sight which will never be forgotten by the hundreds of spellbound spectators who lined the beach. I myself would not have believed it possible for even a strong and young crew to do so much with this heavy boat . . .' He was in no doubt that the greatest credit was due to Coxswain Blogg. 'It was his own remarkable personality and really great qualities of leadership which magnetised tired and somewhat dispirited men into launching, and when the boat was launched it was the consummate skill with which he managed her and the encouragement he gave the crew which brought their efforts to such a successful conclusion.'

Every man aboard the *Louisa Hartwell* lifeboat that day was decorated for gallantry. Blogg received the first of his three gold medals – and later an Empire Gallantry Medal, which would be exchanged for the George Cross, the nation's highest civilian bravery award.

Henry Blogg's unerring ability to defy the odds and pull off the seemingly impossible was reflected not only in the awards showered on him, but in the relentless flood of publicity all around. During his lifetime he was immortalised in print, film and works of art. And there has scarcely been any let-up since his death in 1954, his brilliant career featuring in books, magazines, newspapers and even children's comics.

His impact on the RNLI was immense. According to Edward Wake-Walker, in his study of *Gold Medal Rescues*, 'his exploits off the coast of Norfolk did more than anything else to endear the RNLI to the British public in the first half of the 20th century.'

In 1997, as director of the RNLI, Brian Miles set Blogg alongside the institution's founder, Sir William Hillary, as one of the most important figures in their history. 'Everyone knows his name, and there's no question that he played a big part in raising our profile. We have had many respected coxswains, but Henry Blogg above all others has become an inspiration and an example, and I'm sure his name still acts as a spur and encouragement to present day lifeboatmen.'

Viscount Templewood, president of the Cromer branch of the RNLI, described him memorably as 'one of the bravest men who lived'. The Chief Inspector of Lifeboats, in a tribute broadcast after Blogg's death in 1954, called him 'a kindly, genial man of exemplary character and possessing a youthful spirit; a magnificent seaman with the courage of a lion, a man of quick decisions and resolute action.'

Tributes still flow a half century after his death, but perhaps the finest acknowledgement of Blogg's outstanding qualities came from one of his crew who said on the day of his funeral: 'Had he been in the Navy he would have been an admiral. In the Army he would have been a general. Whatever he chose, he would have been "the guv'nor". He was that type of man.'

3

James Adams (1839–1903)

The First Clergyman to win the Victoria Cross

The Fens flatlands rolling for miles across Norfolk's westernmost borders are worlds away from the desolate mountains of Afghanistan. Yet, in a small brick mission-church on the west bank of the River Ouse, there is a fascinating link between these starkly contrasting countries in the shape of a wooden communion table.

Its place in the sleepy settlement of Stow Bridge, near Downham Market, bears testimony to memories of stirring deeds performed well over a century ago by Norfolk's most remarkable 'Christian soldier', the Rev James William Adams. The simple, unadorned table is the one he carried with him through the yawning canyons of Afghanistan as the only civilian chaplain accompanying the powerful British army of invasion in its three-year campaign that is now called the Second Afghan War. Just as much at home in the saddle as in any parish pulpit, the padre was admired by humble soldier and general alike. During the triumphant march to Kabul he earned numerous mentions in dispatches for his unofficial actions as an additional member of Lord Roberts' staff. His greatest deeds, however, were reserved for the controversial engagement fought out on the wide-open Charder Plain, west of Kabul, in the cold light of a December morning in 1879. His exploits that day would result in unparalleled reward.

Roberts conceived a plan that almost ended in bloody disaster. Designed as a means of trapping and crushing a popular uprising against British rule, it misfired spectacularly. Roberts himself later called it 'a striking exemplification of the uncertainty of war'. He

Padre James Adams VC

claimed his plan would have achieved total success but for his subordinate commander's deviation from his intended route. This resulted in a move which led his small force a few hundred strong into the path of an Afghan army numbering 10,000. Some historians strongly contest that point, maintaining that Roberts' 'master-stroke' was based on faulty intelligence. He set no trap for the vast army because he simply did not know it existed. He expected to meet only about 2,000 dispirited tribesmen.

The two armies collided near the village of Kila Kazi on a plain intersected by streams and watercourses. Roberts had ridden out of camp that morning with Padre Adams who had become his friend and trusted aide, to see for himself the outcome of his plan. Instead, they were almost engulfed by the Afghan advance. Amid the chaos and confusion of a rapid retreat, three artillery pieces fell into a 12 ft deep ditch. Roberts and Adams came upon a wounded cavalryman staggering away from the seething mass of tribesmen.

This moment found the perfect men in these two contrasting characters. While the general barked instructions that were to safely extricate the bulk of his force, the clergyman turned his attention to helping the wounded. Despite the proximity of a huge Afghan army, Adams dismounted and tried to lift the stricken cavalryman onto his charger. Unfortunately he succeeded only in scaring the horse, which galloped away. Refusing to budge, he remained supporting the wounded man until a group of retreating cavalrymen came to his aid. But his work had barely begun. Next, he set out to rescue two men trapped beneath their fallen horses at the edge of the watercourse, directly in front of the exultant Afghans.

Roberts watched all this in utter amazement and later recorded: 'I thought my friend the padre could not possibly escape. I called out to him to look after himself, but he paid no attention to my warnings . . .' Adams, a man of immense strength, succeeded in hauling the two cavalrymen from beneath their mounts while the water around him foamed with crashing hooves and flying bullets. Luckily for them, the Afghans failed to press home their advance at the last moment and the men were able to escape and rejoin the scattered remnants of the force.

When the fighting was over, Roberts had no hesitation in recommending Adams for the Victoria Cross, the nation's highest award for martial valour. However, as a civilian clergyman he was ineligible for the medal, but under pressure from Roberts the rules were altered to allow the padre to become the first man of the cloth to win the VC.

Adams became rector of Postwick, near Norwich, from 1887 to

1895. He then moved to West Norfolk and became rector of Wimbotsham and vicar of Stow Bardolph until he retired in 1902, aged 64. Here he had accepted the living offered him by Sir Thomas Hare. The church of the Holy Trinity in Stow Bardolph may appear on the dull side until you enter the Hare mausoleum, built in brick and full of monuments.

One easily missed in the far corner is a mahogany cupboard that contains the highly eccentric waxwork monument of Sarah Hare. Legend has it she was punished for working on a Sunday, turning her back on convention and doing some sewing. Whether it was divine intervention or sheer lack of concentration, poor Sarah pricked her finger with a pin and died as a result. Before passing away in 1744 she ordered that her memory be not forgotten. So a wax life-size and life-like model of her was made, dressed and mounted in a wall cabinet, and there it remains, staring awesomely and hauntingly real.

Padre Adams' memorial, erected 'by his friend General Roberts' is not in any of these churches. It is actually in one that was not even built during his lifetime. Stow Bridge, part of the parish of Stow Bardolph, had no church of its own during his ministry. So for the benefit of far-flung parishioners on the edge of the Fens he travelled to Stow Bridge to hold services in the village school, using the same portable altar table that he had carried with him on active service. When the mission church was built there in 1908, five years after his death, his widow donated the much-travelled altar, together with the credence table he used with it, and both of them are still in use today.

4

Thomas Bilney (1495–1531)

The Norfolk Martyr

A frail young priest from a Norfolk village went to his cruel fate with a serene smile on his face and true forgiveness in his heart. Thomas Bilney was burned at the stake in Norwich on Saturday, 19th August 1531. He gave his life willingly so the country might be freed from idolatry and superstition. He was a martyr later hailed as 'the light of dawn in England's night of darkness' and a faithful forerunner of the Reformation.

It seems remarkable now that Bilney, so meek and tender-minded, should be condemned to burn as a heretic, even in times when such events were not uncommon. His doctrines differed little from those of the authorities who put him to death – and only two years after his demise some of those beliefs were adopted in England following Henry VIII's break with Rome. Ordained in 1519, he had largely accepted the Rome position, but he didn't believe in the mediation of saints between man and God or in the worship of relics.

Pilgrimages to Canterbury could do nothing for the soul. The idolatry of Christendom had kept the Jews from Christ. These beliefs were at the heart of the Lollards' movement, a powerful religious movement that had emerged as a force during the 14th and 15th centuries. Its members sought more freedom of religious thought and the right to interpret the Bible for themselves. This brought them into conflict with the religious establishment. And that was one step away from a clash with the political establishment, with the King, and therefore an act of treason.

Thomas Bilney on the village sign at East Bilney

Persecution was particularly intense in London and the Eastern Counties. Bilney died in flames in the Lollards' Pit in Norwich, close to the river at Bishop's Bridge in a low valley surrounded by rising woodland and so forming a sort of amphitheatre.

So how did this diminutive figure from a scattered parish in the middle of Norfolk rise to such significance in Tudor England? He was born in East Bilney, five miles north-west of Dereham (not to be confused with the village of West Bilney, seven miles south-east of King's Lynn). His home was possibly the fine timber house now known as Martyr's Cottage, which according to local legend belonged to Bilney's parents. He went to Cambridge to study law as an undergraduate of Trinity Hall, then was ordained to St Bartholomew's Priory at Smithfield in London, returning to Cambridge in 1520 to become a fellow of Trinity Hall.

Bilney then began a long search for spiritual peace, and became a central figure among a group of reformed theologians who met regularly at Cambridge's White Horse Inn. Though a slender, small and insignificant-looking man, he exerted considerable influence over his colleagues. He prayed most earnestly for Bishop Hugh Latimer, who had denounced Bilney and the others of this group who studied the scriptures. But one of the most astonishing conversions recorded in history followed.

Bilney went to Latimer and asked him to hear his confession. Latimer may have thought Bilney, the Bible fanatic, had seen the error of his ways and was anxious to return to the bosom of the church. However, the priest's fervent testimony penetrated to the very heart of Latimer's convictions and he wept bitterly as he saw 'the truth of the Word of God' and the obstinate war he had waged on God through his own practices. Latimer remained seated as Bilney rose from his knees and consoled him saying, 'Brother, though your sins be as scarlet, they shall be as white as snow'. The two thus became inseparable friends and both in turn became martyrs for their faith. Latimer, along with Nicholas Ridley, was burned at the stake in Oxford in 1555 during the reign of 'Bloody' Mary.

Bilney was twice arrested, imprisoned in the Tower of London for a spell and ordered by Cardinal Wolsey to recant his reformed faith. He did agree to stop preaching his doctrines, but could not bottle up the faith within him for very long.

He set off for what proved to be a fatal preaching tour of Norfolk in 1531. It is about this time that we get a thumbnail portrait of 'Little Bilney' from some of his Cambridge followers. He was seen as a man 'in delicate health, who observed a severe diet, taking but one meal a day and never sleeping more than four hours, absorbed in prayer and in the study of the Word, displaying at all times all the energy of charity.'

On arrival in his home county, Bilney was not allowed to use churches so he preached in the open air. However, he was soon arrested in Norwich by Bishop Nykke, tried, and sentenced. On the eve of his execution Bilney was composed and joyful. It is said that after eating his final meal, he rose and placed his finger in the flame of a lamp. He only withdrew it when the first joint had been burnt, and quietly recited the words of Isaiah: 'When thou walkest through the fire, thou shalt not be burned; neither shall the flame kindle upon thee.'

Bilney passed through the packed city streets the next morning, his features calm, his head shaved and wearing a layman's gown. Several monks who had given evidence against him, sizing up the emotion of the crowd, started to tremble and whispered in panic to the little man: 'These people will believe that we are the cause of your death, and will withhold their alms.' So Bilney turned to the noisy throng and said: 'Good folks, be not angry against these men for my sake: even should they be the authors of my death, it is not they.'

Of Bilney's last moments, John Foxe wrote in his *Book of Martyrs*: 'Then the officers put reeds and faggots about his body and set fire to them, which made a very great flame, and deformed his face, he holding up his hands and knocking upon his breast, saying sometimes "Jesus!", sometimes "I believe!".

'The flame was blown away from him by the violence of the wind which was that day, and two or three days before very great; and so for a little pause he stood without flame; but soon the wood again took the flame, and then he gave up the ghost and his body being withered, bowed downward against the chain. Then one of the officers with his halberd smote out the staple in the stake behind him and suffered his body to fall into the bottom of the fire, laying wood on it; and so he was consumed.'

Tradition has it that his ashes were taken back to East Bilney and laid in the churchyard. A sexton is said to have dug up the urn containing them and then buried them again – but no one knows precisely where. In St Mary's church there is an 1885 window on the south side in rich dark colours, which commemorates this parish's most famous son. It shows him with his Bible, preaching, and then chained to the burning stake, with Norwich Cathedral in the background.

5

Fanny Burney (1752–1840)

Novelist, Diarist and Royal Courtier

Fanny Burney moved in the most brilliant social and literary circles of her time. She was a novelist, diarist, playwright, and courtier to George III and Queen Charlotte, and she witnessed the Battle of Waterloo. Her portrait in London's National Portrait Gallery hangs alongside those of Dr Johnson, Laurence Sterne and David Garrick; fitting company for the girl from King's Lynn who recorded contemporary events and the people around them with wit and clarity in her journals and letters.

She lived for 88 years, from the age of Johnson until the age of Dickens. At 8 she had been dismissed as a dunce. Following the death of her mother in September 1762, her father remarried some five years later and at 15 Fanny decided she would 'never be happy'. Yet in 1778, at 26, her first and most successful novel, *Evelina*, was published and acclaimed as an enormous triumph. She became the toast of fashionable London.

One evening in 1779, Fanny was chatting to the artist Sir Joshua Reynolds at a soirée when the playwright Richard Brinsley Sheridan joined them. Having just enjoyed *Evelina*, he said he would take any comedy she wrote, sight unseen, for Drury Lane. So she wrote a comedy, four in fact, although it wasn't until the summer of 2000 that one of them made its West End debut. *A Busy Day* pokes fun at the clash between the emerging City nouveau riche and the landed aristocracy.

Fanny was born in King's Lynn, one of the many children of talented musician Dr Charles Burney and his first wife Esther. She

FANNY BURNEY (1752–1840)

St Margaret's church, King's Lynn, where Fanny Burney's father, Dr Charles Burney, was organist

lived as a child in a house facing the west end of St Margaret's church, where her father was organist, and later spent summers in the town after the family had returned to London. Fanny rose early and went for walks in the fields around Lynn because there was nobody about then. It was impossible to do likewise in London 'for fear of robbers – but here everybody is known and one has nothing to apprehend.' However, she loathed the social life of Lynn's upper-class families: 'Such a set of tittle tattle prittle prattle visitants! Oh fear! I am sick of the ceremony and fuss of these dull people!'

King's Lynn was known as Lynn Regis when the family settled there a year or so before Fanny's birth. Poor health had forced Dr Burney to leave the smoky, dank atmosphere of London where he had made considerable marks as both performer and composer.

But he was appalled at having to leave behind a flourishing career in the capital to retire, at only 25, to a provincial market town. Even today many grumble about the way the Burneys denigrated the town – and no plaque adorns the home where Fanny spent her first years. Her father's comments about the congregation's 'total ignorance of the most known and common musical merits' still rankle, as does his condemnation of the organ in St Margaret's. He disliked the instrument so much that he persuaded the parish to import a fine organ from Germany. It is still in use.

Baptised in the 15th century chapel of St Nicholas – the largest chapel of ease in England and one of the two attached to the old priory church of St Margaret's – Fanny returned to Lynn throughout her formative years to stay at Dower House, near the churchyard of St Margaret's, with Mrs Stephen Allen, who later became her stepmother. She learned to read and write quite late, but by 10 she was conjuring up short stories and keeping a diary. No doubt alarmed by her stepmother's warning that to be known as a 'scribbler' would seriously harm her marriage prospects, 15 year old Fanny burnt her romantic manuscripts and resolved to write only her journal. Happily, she was unable to keep her pledge and eleven years later, in 1778, *Evelina* was published and was a instant success.

She wrote in her diary: 'My little book, I am told, is now at all the circulating libraries. I have an exceeding odd sensation when I consider it is now in the power of any and every body to read what I so carefully hoarded even from my best friends until the last month or two; and that a work which was so lately lodged in all privacy in my bureau may now be seen by every butcher and baker, cobbler and tinker throughout the three kingdoms for the small tribute of threepence.' It is thought she collected a mere £20 for *Evelina*. Interestingly, a copy of the book fetched £4,000 in 1930! For her next volume, *Cecilia*, she received £250 – an

FANNY BURNEY (1752–1840)

Portrait of Fanny Burney by Sir Joshua Reynolds

indication of her standing in the literary world. Fanny avoided the obvious route into high society for a well-brought-up young lady which was to make a convenient marriage. Observing a wedding party as a demure 16 year old she remarked: 'How short a time does it take to put an eternal end to a woman's liberty!'

Then at 40 she fell in love with a French refugee, General Alexandre d'Arblay. He was not exactly a glittering catch from her family's point of view, given the political situation and the fact that the d'Arblay estates had been seized in the Revolution. But they married within months and Fanny gave birth to her only child, a son, at 42.

By the time of her marriage she had already spent five years bored to distraction in the Royal Household as Second Keeper of the Robes to Queen Charlotte, a position she was invited to take up on the strength of her fame as author of *Evelina*. It was during this time that Fanny was hailed by the mad King George III in the garden of Kew Palace. She ran, terrified: 'I protest I was ready to die. I knew not in what state he might be at the time. I only knew the orders to keep out of his way were universal.' In the event, he was in a benign mood and kissed her warmly on the cheek. Fanny's journal of life at court has provided valuable first-hand information about the King's illness and its effect on the entire household.

Fanny outlived both her husband and son, but in 1811 she underwent a mastectomy without anaesthetic, which she recorded in chilling detail for her sister Hetty. Only the day after the operation she was sitting up taking chicken broth. She lived for 29 more years.

Admired by Sheridan, Dr Johnson and Jane Austen (who is said to have found the title for *Pride and Prejudice* in her novel *Cecilia*), Fanny Burney also provided Thackeray with material. His account of the massing of troops before Waterloo in *Vanity Fair* is based on her journals. Her comedies of domestic life, designed around innocent heroines as they enter a sophisticated world, prefigure Jane Austen and cast Fanny as one of the most influential women writers in our language. The 20th century author, editor and critic Walter Allen wrote: 'To read Miss Burney is rather like having a mouse's view of the world of cats; the cats are very terrifying, but the mouse's sense of the ridiculous could not be keener.' Although the immense success of *Evelina*, a tale of love and fluctuating family fortunes, was never to be fully repeated, she thoroughly deserved the description of 'a real wonder' from Dr Johnson.

6

Edith Cavell (1865–1915)

'Patriotism is Not Enough'

Secret documents, released the best part of a century after her death, show how Norfolk's First World War heroine knew she was being stalked by German spies months before they arrested her for helping Allied soldiers. But despite Edith Cavell's desperate pleas for help in secret letters sent back home, the British authorities were unable to save her. She was executed for alleged espionage in October 1915. The MI5 documents, made public for the first time in 2002, give a chilling insight into how the brave nurse became aware that the net was closing in and her life was in danger.

Edith was born in Swardeston, four miles south-west of Norwich, where her father Frederick was vicar for nearly 46 years. As a child, Edith loved to pick and draw the many wild flowers on the common as they came into season. She presented friends with delicate paintings of roses or animals, several of which are still kept and treasured.

Becoming a nurse, she later ran a nursing school in Brussels. When war broke out and Belgium fell to the Germans, she secretly helped British, French and Belgian soldiers escape to rejoin the fight. Correspondence shows that by the summer before her capture, Edith became aware the Germans were on her trail and she sent a message back to Britain via a Belgian aristocrat, Count de Borchgrave. In a letter to her mother in Norwich, she warned of a German undercover agent operating in both Belgium and England. This man had a 'reddish face, fair, short military moustache and a real cockney accent', and had threatened to track down Mrs Cavell and interrogate her about her daughter's activities. However, the warning only reached the British on 1st August – five days before Edith was imprisoned by the Germans.

The new evidence shows that, on receiving Edith's warning, de Borchgrave wrote to his wife, then living in Berkshire. He also enclosed a letter to be passed to Edith's mother. His wife immediately contacted the authorities, and on 1st August she was interviewed by Superintendent Charles Goddard of Wokingham police: 'The Countess states that her husband is in Brussels and he has written to say that it is extremely dangerous for a British woman to be within the country occupied by the German army.

'She, the Countess, was to caution Mrs Cavell that if she talks to people about her, it may get known to the Germans, and if it does there is no telling what might be her fate,' reported Superintendent Goddard.

On 8th August the letter was forwarded to Mrs Cavell by police in Norwich. But for her daughter Edith it was already too late. She had been arrested three days earlier after being betrayed by an informant. Special Branch tried to track down the German with the 'reddish face and real cockney accent', who had also claimed to have a florist's shop in Forest Hill, south London, but they were not successful.

When de Borchgrave returned to England that November, he told MI5 how the German agent together with two other plain clothes officers, had been there when he visited Edith's house in the Rue de la Culture just two weeks before her arrest. Early next morning, the Count had been visited by a young English girl with a message from Edith to be passed on as quickly as possible to her mother and to the British Consul in Rotterdam. 'The message was not to give any info about Miss Cavell and to be careful of spies, especially this man with the red face,' de Borchgrave explained to MI5. 'He had told Miss Cavell that he went to England whenever he wanted and that he would do so and see

Mrs Cavell and the Belgian Consul in Rotterdam and get all the info he required. I do not think the man's statement was merely bluff.'

By the time of the Count's interview with MI5, Edith was already dead. She had been executed on 12th October for harbouring enemy servicemen – despite appeals from the Vatican and the United States, and despite the fact she had not been involved in espionage. The death sentence deeply angered the head of MI5, Colonel Vernon Kell, who said Britain must now be prepared to exact the same penalty on any female German spies that fell into their hands. 'We are dealing with an unscrupulous enemy who apparently does not even require evidence of espionage in order to execute a woman,' he said. When the British obtained a photograph of her grave, Colonel Kell personally sent her mother a copy.

Edith Cavell remained calm and dignified throughout her hasty trial. Princess Marie de Croy, one of the leaders of the Belgian resistance, who stood in the dock with her, was asked in cross examination if she did not realise the dangers she ran in acting so. A contemporary writer recalls: 'The Princess, petite, slim, looking ill, replied firmly and proudly: "One must do one's duty without thinking of the consequences." She it was who, without consideration for her own safety, told the court that Nurse Cavell was brought into danger because she, the Princess, and her compatriots had sent men to her to hide them. With supreme selflessness she pleaded: "If anyone should be punished, it should be us, not her."'

However, while the Princess survived a German prison and the war, the nurse from Norfolk did not. She was sentenced to the firing squad. Rising on her last morning at 5 o'clock, when the British chaplain visited her, she met him in her dressing gown. The words she spoke to him in her cell summed up her character and have reverberated proudly down the years: 'Standing as I do in view of God and Eternity, I realise that patriotism is not enough. I must have no hatred or bitterness towards anyone.' We are told that she then walked 'quietly and calmly down the gloomy corridor to her death, Belgian soldiers bowing deeply as she passed.'

The outcry that followed the nurse's execution simply astonished the German government. They had made a serious error of judgement and her death helped to bring America into the war. Propaganda about her death caused recruitment to double for eight weeks after the news had been broken. The Kaiser himself ordered that in future no woman was to be shot without his personal consent.

With the end of the war, Belgium and France showered Miss Cavell posthumously with honours. Her body was exhumed and guarded by the Belgian army across Flanders to Ostend. Then she was given into the care of the Royal Navy and at Dover the coffin was borne ashore by naval ratings. A gun carriage drew her through London to Westminster Abbey, where the first part of the funeral service was intoned. From there she was brought back to Norwich and to the county that had nurtured her. The body was carried into the Cathedral Close by army officers, among them some she had helped to escape.

Bishop Pollock described her as 'alive in God' and she was laid to rest outside the cathedral in a spot called Life's Green. Here services are held annually on the Saturday closest to the anniversary of her death. A flower festival is also held every year in her memory in her home village of Swardeston, where a corner of St Mary's church has been put aside for her portrait, showing her seated with her dogs Don and Jack, and a portion of the plain wooden cross returned from her grave at the rifle range in Brussels where she met her fate. The village sign also bears her likeness. Her home patch welcomes many visitors each year, including several from Brussels where she pioneered her training

Edith Cavell is carried into Norwich Cathedral

of nurses and cared for the sick and distressed.

'I am just a nurse who tried to do her duty,' was Edith Cavell's gloriously modest description of herself. She did not look for martyrdom. She knew the import of what she had done – and was ready to pay the price.

7

John Crome (1768–1821)

A Master Painter

The founder and father figure of the world-famous Norwich School of Painting, John Crome stands out in the history of British art as an artist of national stature but without national ambitions.

He was content to stay in his native city although remarkable talents in both oils and watercolour would have allowed him to take London by storm. A superb technician, he had studied closely the great landscape painters of the Netherlands. Their influence is clearly felt in Crome's choice of subject matter – townscapes, night scenes and village views. But he was no simple imitator, with some of his work startlingly original.

The Norwich Society was formed in 1803 to institute 'An Enquiry into the Rise, Progress and Present State of Painting, Architecture and Sculpture, with a view to point out the Best Methods of Study to attain Greater Perfection in the Arts.' That prepared the ground for the Norwich School of Painters, established virtually single-handed by Crome, a modest, gentle and charming man who was made welcome in every household at all levels of society. Though the art world was then small in London, it was even smaller in Norwich and almost every painter of that period in Norwich either trained under Crome or knew him and his work.

In 1806 Crome exhibited his first two paintings at the Royal Academy. He was known as Old Crome by the time he was 43 for he had three sons, all of whom became painters. In the magnificent large canvasses *Mousehold Heath* and *Poringland Oak*, which both hang in the Tate, we see Crome in his prime. Sadly in April 1821, while working on a preliminary sketch for a painting of the Yarmouth Water Frolic, he went down with a fever and died within a fortnight.

There's a memorial to him in the church of St George, Colegate, in Norwich, where he is buried in the south aisle chapel. The memorial, erected 47 years after his death, is inscribed: 'Near this spot lie the remains of one of England's greatest landscape painters born in this city, December 22, 1768, and died in this parish April 22, 1821.' But his true memorials hang today all over the world, and there is a superb collection in Norwich Castle Museum.

Crome began life in an alehouse kept by his father, who also worked as a journeyman weaver. *The Griffin* was in Conisford Street (now King Street). Young Crome began to earn his scanty living as a signpainter's apprentice, learning at an early age to grind and mix colours and to apply oil paint to canvas or panel. Then he landed a job as drawing master after being befriended by Thomas Harvey of Catton, who was a wealthy member of a notable Norwich family and had his own private gallery of masterpieces. Before long Crome attained the post of drawing master to the influential Gurney family at Earlham, soon putting behind him this description when aged 20: 'a very awkward, uninformed county lad but extremely shrewd in all his remarks upon art, though he wanted words and terms to express his meaning.'

Writer George Borrow was only too willing to sing Crome's praises, especially to fellow artists. In one enthusiastic outburst of typically colourful language he exclaimed: 'A living master? Why there he comes! Thou has had him long, he has long guided thy young hand towards the excellence which is yet far from thee, but which thou canst attain if thou should persist and wrestle, even as he has done, midst gloom and despondency – ay, and

JOHN CROME (1768–1821)

John Crome, from a portrait by Hannah Gurney

even contempt; he who now comes up the creaking stairs to thy little studio in the second floor to inspect thy last efforts before thou departest; the little stout man whose face is very dark, and whose eye is vivacious; that man has attained excellence, destined some day to be acknowledged, though not till he is cold and his mortal part returned to its kindred clay.

'He has painted, not pictures of the world but English pictures, such as Gainsborough himself might have done; beautiful rural pictures, with trees which might well tempt the little birds to perch upon them; thou needst not run to Rome, brother, after pictures of the world whilst at home there are pictures of England, nor needst thou even go to London, the big city, in search of a master, for thou hast one at home in the old East Anglian town who can instruct thee whilst thou needest instruction; better stay at home, brother, at least for a season, and toil and strive midst groaning and despondency till thou has attained excellence even as he has done . . . the little dark man with the brown coat and the top-boots, whose name will one day be considered the chief ornament of the old town, and whose works will at no distant period rank amongst the proudest pictures of England – and England against the world! – thy master, my brother, thy, at present all too little considered, master CROME!'

This is a trifle over the top, perhaps, but gives an indication of how highly influential people measured his importance, not least as a 'stay-at-home' genius, as individual and sturdily independent as the Norwich and Norfolk he loved. John Crome was behind the genesis and inspiration of the Norwich School, the one important school of painting to take its name and character from a city and its surroundings. Almost his whole life and work were influenced by the city and its immediate countryside. He was not drawn to London or the Continent like so many others, and nor did he seek fashionable patronage.

JOHN CROME (1768–1821)

Yarmouth Beach by John Crome

Crome did not paint more than 300 pictures as much of his time was taken up with teaching. His son, John Berney Crome, George Vincent and James Stark followed most closely in his footsteps. Some say their work is almost indistinguishable to the casual eye from that of Old Crome himself. Certainly the four of them caught the charm of old Norwich and the forest-like beauty of its surrounding woods.

8

George Edwards (1850–1933)

Rural Trade Unionist and Son of the Soil

The scrawny but determined boy, not yet six years old, started work just after sunrise. He shouted loudly and waved a stick to frighten birds from the corn. It went on like that until sunset, scaring crows to help the meagre family budget. His first weekly wage saw him running home clutching a whole shilling. He gave it to his mother with a proud smile: 'Now we shall not want for bread any more, and you will not have to cry again. You shall always have my money. I will always look after you.'

George Edwards was determined even then to make a difference in the world about him, a world soaked in poverty, hardship and tears. His father, a farm labourer, had been in prison for taking turnips from his employer's field. The rest of the family had to go into the workhouse, a familiar fate in Victorian Norfolk where wages were low and hours of labour long.

The inspiring story of one of the key characters in the history of rural trade unionism led from crow scaring to Westminster when George became an MP at the age of 70. He was knighted ten years later, a remarkable achievement for someone born in abject poverty and who received no education worth talking about. He was still unable to read or write when he married, but his wife Charlotte became his teacher when he heeded the call to organise the downtrodden labourers. She would say with conviction: 'You make the effort. I'll make the sacrifice.' When he became a preacher on the Aylsham Primitive Methodist circuit, Charlotte taught him the scripture lessons and hymns by rote.

GEORGE EDWARDS (1850–1933)

George Edwards

In the month after his name appeared on the circuit plan, George met Joseph Arch, himself a Primitive Methodist preacher and founder of the first national trade union for agricultural labourers. From this time onwards George became deeply involved in union matters. He saw his union and preaching activities as complementary to each other. 'With my study of theology I soon began to realise that the social conditions of the people were not as God intended they should be.'

The grim year of 1874 saw strikes and lock-outs throughout East Anglia and beyond, with 10,000 men losing their jobs simply for belonging to a union. George wrote of that time: 'In the village where I lived I preached my first Labour sermon.' The Third Reform Bill of 1884 at last gave agricultural labourers the vote, and the following year Joseph Arch became MP for West Norfolk. Even so, rural trade unionism, hit by yet another agricultural depression, was in serious decline.

After the 1906 election, in which the Conservatives suffered a resounding defeat, many labourers lost their jobs and their tied cottage homes on suspicion of harbouring radical views or having voted Liberal. George was approached by Norfolk labourers to found a new union, and the Eastern Counties Agricultural Workers and Small Holders Union, later to become the National Union of Agricultural Workers, was formed. The Edwards stock continued to rise, and in a by-election in July 1920 George was elected Labour MP for South Norfolk with a majority of over 2,000. His maiden speech, a plea for action to tackle the problem of unemployment in rural areas, ended with the words: 'In Heaven's name, find them work!' One newspaper report referred to his 'earth-clodden sentences'.

Agricultural depression in the early 1920s again forced down wages causing great hardship in the countryside, and, in 1923, precipitated a national strike. Union historian Reg Groves writes: 'Old George Edwards was everywhere, on the platform, on committees, or leading the men's representations in negotiations.' A settlement was reached which guaranteed a wage of 25 shillings for a 50-hour week. Already honoured with an OBE, 'Old George' became 'Sir George' when he was knighted by George V in June 1930.

Despite failing health, he remained active in local politics. On 22nd November 1933 he attended a meeting of the Board of Guardians of Thursford Workhouse where he urged that something should be done for a land worker and his wife threatened with eviction. This was his last public engagement. He

The cottage at Marsham, near Aylsham, where George Edwards was born

died the following Wednesday at his Fakenham home. Following the funeral service in Fakenham Methodist church, all businesses were closed as the cortège headed for Fakenham cemetery and the streets were lined with people from all walks of life. Outside the Queen's Road School near the cemetery, children stood with teachers to pay their last respects to one who had championed the cause of youth in the town and also served their interests on the county education committee.

The union founded by Sir George remained an important influence in the life of the countryside until, with falling membership as the number of men employed in agriculture diminished, it was amalgamated in 1982 with the Transport and General Workers Union. Throughout much of its history the union maintained close links with the Methodist Church, and in the early days many officers gained their initial public speaking and organisational skills in the village chapels. Union 'church parades' were held in Methodist churches until the 1950s.

A service of remembrance and wreath-laying at George Edwards' memorial is held annually at Fakenham cemetery, while his connections with the town are represented on the town sign by a plough. There's a plaque on his birthplace, a cottage at Marsham, a few yards from the main Aylsham to Norwich road. Until modernisation in the 1970s, two red bricks at the rear remained with the name of Mary, George's mother, and '1859' still decipherable. There's also an annual memorial lecture in the former workhouse chapel at Roots, the rural life museum at Gressenhall, near East Dereham. It is a true mark of his work and dedication that his name is still so revered and ranked in the history of Norfolk agriculture alongside 'Turnip' Townshend and Thomas William Coke, aristocrats, who were great improvers of the land.

One of the most telling tributes to George Edwards came at the graveside when his old friend Walter Smith made a parting address in honour of 'one of Norfolk's greatest sons . . . though he was gentle with those who had injured him personally, he displayed indignation and passion for the wrongs that his fellows suffered. He spoke with a force and eloquence never excelled on the village green and seldom on the platform . . . he had great courage. He feared no man. We will try to carry on to a completed finish the work to which he gave the whole of his devoted life.'

9

Ted Ellis (1909–1986)

Naturalist and Broadcaster

An expert without airs, a celebrity who remained a modest man, Ted Ellis eagerly shared his remarkable knowledge as naturalist and broadcaster with a wide audience of all ages. His twinkling sense of humour and refreshingly natural style made him one of Norfolk's best-loved characters of the 20th century – no mean achievement for a lad born in the Channel Islands!

'Having feasted my senses on the wonders of nature since I was a toddler, the countryside wherever I have happened to be has been a never-failing source of interest and delight' . . . that's how he summed up his career shortly before his death in 1986. Dr Tony Irwin, Keeper of Natural History at Norwich Castle Museum, said: 'I don't think there is going to be his like again. His breadth of knowledge has never been equalled, and our knowledge of natural history in Norfolk is down to Ted.'

He was a pioneer in the field of conservation long before it became fashionable. A self-taught scientist, he had the joy of nature constantly shining in his eyes, vividly describing the world of Norfolk fens and waterways, explaining the complex ways in which one life-form depends upon another and exploring the need to protect and conserve the area's richness. For 40 years he lived with his family at Wheatfen Broad, Surlingham, in a remote cottage by a reedy wilderness – a naturalist's paradise a few miles east of Norwich. After his death, his energetic widow Phyllis led the campaign to turn Wheatfen Broad into a permanent nature reserve through the Ted Ellis Trust.

Ted Ellis

TED ELLIS

Born in Guernsey of Norfolk parents, he was fascinated in childhood by the 'rich adventures' of discovering the natural world. He came to Norfolk when he was 10 and soon enjoyed the friendship and help of older naturalists in Yarmouth, each imbued with enthusiasm for their special study, whether it was of birds, plants, insects, microscopic pond life or the treasures of the sea. Doyen of them all was Arthur Henry Patterson, who wrote under the gloriously self-effacing name of John Knowlittle.

Young Ted became his disciple: 'In the years of our companionship he opened up new vistas by introducing me to the mudflats of Breydon and many of his favourite haunts on the Broads. He not only gave me courage to seek a career as a naturalist, but offered succinct advice on putting pen to paper.' Patterson wrote numerous books on the natural history of East Norfolk and for many years his nature notes, illustrated by lively sketches, delighted readers of the local newspapers. The old man maintained that a true naturalist should always be ready to share his pleasures with others. If communication was the Patterson gospel, it was certainly the Ellis gift.

Ted was Keeper of Natural History at Norwich Castle Museum from 1928 until 1956. Most of his spare time was spent taking part in activities of natural history societies and the Norfolk Naturalists' Trust. Although investigating and recording details of the flora and fauna of East Anglia and other regions absorbed his attention, he never lost that sense of wonder and delight of adventuring in wild places in all weathers, day and night, season by season. In 1946 he began daily contributions to the *Eastern Daily Press* under the 'Countryside' heading, and in 1964 he became a regular writer for the *Guardian*'s 'A Country Diary'. Those initials E.A.E. became the trademark for unmissable breakfast reading in Norfolk and way beyond.

Then Ted found a new audience as a popular radio and television broadcaster. His 15-minute 'Nature Postbag' on BBC

Radio 4 Midland in the 1960s was estimated to have attracted a million listeners on one occasion. There were many national broadcasts and Ted was appointed natural history consultant for television, assisting with programmes such as the nationally-networked *Nature Trail*. Then, in 1980, he was invited to take part in a new regional television series called *Weekend* – and his face as well as his voice became famous. With John Mountford as presenter, it turned into one of the most popular TV programmes in the country. In the early 1980s Ted's regular audience was estimated at half a million. He often turned up for television broadcasts with his own scenery – boxes of reeds, bushes, grass and plants – staggering into the studio like a walking fen. Receptionists were always relieved to see him, however, for it wasn't only letters that arrived in Ted's postbag. He was sent matchboxes with beetles in them, strange parcels that rustled if you put your ear close to them, jamjars of ants, spiders of every shape, size and colour, decaying pieces of vegetation – not to mention fish, fungi, frogs, feathers and fossils. Trouble was, Ted only came in once a week!

In August 1982, he was awarded the Royal Television Society's regional prize for his contribution to television over 20 years. It was in another field, however, that he gained the award that stood out as the highlight of his life. It came in 1970 – fittingly, European Conservation Year – when three separate departments at the University of East Anglia recommended him for an honorary doctorate. That triple nomination marked the academic recognition which scientists had privately given him for years. Ted, who left elementary school at 15 without an examination success to his name, became Dr E.A. Ellis.

Two months after his death in July 1986, the Norfolk Naturalists' Trust and the Norfolk and Norwich Naturalists' Society awarded him the first-ever Sydney Long Memorial Medal to mark his 'unique knowledge of natural history in Norfolk'. It was a medal created in honour of one of his old teachers, the same Dr Long who first took him bird-watching at Scolt Head Island.

The funeral at St Mary's parish church in Surlingham was conducted as a celebration, with none of the mourners in black. Half a mile away, along a grassy track, stand the ruins of another church, St Saviour's. They are on a small hill overlooking the Yare Valley, a bird sanctuary and a broad sweep of fenland. Ted was buried there in the first grave for 200 years. At the end of October 1986 there was a second service, this time in Norwich Cathedral, the contrast in scale perfectly illustrating the two lives of Ted Ellis, a simple man with an international reputation. The congregation consisted of over 800 friends, dignitaries and eminent scientists from all over the world. The clergy wore scarlet, the colour of celebration, in a service of thanksgiving.

10

Sidney Grapes (1888–1958)

Rustic Comedian and Champion of Norfolk's dialect

The most endearing and enduring of local characters, rustic comedian Sidney Grapes lit the lantern for a whole generation of performers to illuminate the true Norfolk way. He naturally combined spoken and written entertainments in a lasting style, and his legacy is rich and inspirational. Indeed, his written work has attracted academic interest at the highest level and so added considerable weight to the campaign against directing the Norfolk dialect towards the obituary columns.

Sidney, who lived all his life in the Broadland village of Potter Heigham, had made his mark as the archetypal country comedian at local concerts and dinners well before he dropped a few lines to the morning newspaper, the *Eastern Daily Press*, in January 1946, and over the next twelve years found himself reaching and enthralling a far wider audience. The Boy John Letters, all the more eagerly anticipated because they were irregular, were written in Norfolk dialect but never swamped by it. Sidney wrote as he spoke and spelt as he pleased, taking liberal advantage of the fact that there are no firm rules in the use of phonetics.

The cast list of his articles soon became household names – Boy John, Granfar, Aunt Agatha and the cantankerous Ole Mrs W-. Many readers, myself included when I discovered them as a schoolboy in the early 1950s, used to cheat and turn to the PS first for Aunt Agatha's latest example of home-spun philosophy. Favourites are still constantly exchanged whenever Norfolk people meet and mingle and want to break the ice, from cocktail

SIDNEY GRAPES (1888–1958)

Sidney Grapes

parties to darts club outings – 'PS: Aunt Agatha, she say: "Thass no good a' puttin' yar foot down if yew hint got a leg ter stand on."'

Early letters had readers guessing who some of the characters might be in real life – especially Mrs W – and they were full of post-war austerity as rationing and shortages drew heavy sighs. Even so, a warming humour culled from the very heart of country life shone through from the start and these gems were cut out and sent all over the world to Norfolk exiles.

Those of us raised on such homely humour – and Sidney easily transferred his stagecraft into print – can hardly believe they are half a century old, especially when audiences tumble under their spell at harvest suppers, village socials or family reunions. The appeal still goes much deeper than a refreshing dip into nostalgic waters. Collections of these letters continue to sell in their thousands, underlining their abiding attraction. They may be rooted in time and place but they retain genuine charm and value.

Sidney started work at 15 for his father, a carpenter and builder at Potter Heigham. A bicycle shop developed into a garage and motor business with the increase in traffic to the Broads and the coast. Sidney was the first to accept that holiday traffic weakened the dialect even if it did boost the economy. He lived with his wife Ella in a little flat above the garage. They called it Uptop. On stage he wore an old 'chummy' hat – a soft felt hat with a narrow brim – a smock and a 'ropper' round his neck. But those tempted to dismiss him as just another country bumpkin with a few tales to tell soon discovered he wasn't such a fool as he might have looked.

He would get the audience laughing at him halfway through a yarn, and then up would come the admonishing finger – 'Now, hold yew hard, tergether!' – and he would proceed to the cream of the joke, in which the native triumphed, and soon had the audience laughing with him.

While plaudits close to home have followed the Boy John Letters down the years, helping to turn curiosity into adulation at many a local function, it was a remarkable cultural coup when they were praised a few years ago at a conference in Helsinki! Peter Trudgill, Professor of English Linguistics at the University of Fribourg in Switzerland – and an international expert in the field of dialect – described the Letters as 'work of not a little genius . . . not only are the characterisations and vignettes of village life brilliant and therefore enormously popular, but Sidney

Grapes is also a superb writer of the local dialect, right down to subtleties such as Granfar speaking in a more conservative, traditional way than the other characters.'

Yes, Professor Trudgill is a proud Norfolk lad and president of Friends Of Norfolk Dialect, the flourishing body set up in 1999 to promote and preserve the vernacular. But his scrutiny of the close link between language and society is seen as a key weapon in the battle against a culturally standardised world.

While humour is a key component in Norfolk's continuing struggle to 'dew diffrunt', the professor warns that if dialects are to survive they must be used in as wide a range of contexts as possible: 'The Norfolk dialect is a vital means of helping preserve Norfolk values, culture, way of life. It is also important, more than many other dialects, since it is one of the last dialects in the south of England, and especially the south-east of England, to remain relatively distinctive and relatively widely spoken.'

I doubt if Sidney Grapes expected to be in the front line of such a campaign when he composed that first letter and posted it to the local paper in 1946. However, it blazed such a telling trail that his influence was bound to be felt long after the final epistle was printed in April 1958. Eric Fowler, who wrote with great flair and distinction for the *Eastern Daily Press* as Jonathan Mardle, recalled that offstage Sidney had little more than an ordinary tincture of Norfolk in his speech, 'but the important point about him was that Norfolk was his native tongue. He was village born and bred. He knew intimately the sort of people he was writing about and met them every day.'

Sidney lived through sweeping changes in his home village. Potter Heigham grew into one of the three capitals of the Broads' holiday trade and boating industry. Along with Wroxham on the Bure and Oulton Broad on the Waveney, Potter flourished as Herbert Woods, who built his first motor cruiser in 1925, developed the biggest fleet on the Broads. Of course, Sidney added to the village's fame after the Second World War with the Boy John Letters and his reputation as an entertainer. Older inhabitants still call it the Boy John's village, and a new development called Grapes Close serves to keep his name to the fore. It is in the beautiful parish church, however, that his memory burns the brightest.

The older part of St Nicholas' church, with its round, flint tower and thatched roof of Broadland reed, dates back to the 12th century. By Sidney's wishes, it was decorated at his funeral as if for a spring festival and joyful hymns were sung. Later in the year an oak-panelled clergy vestry was built and dedicated to his memory – in this lovely place where he had been a chorister from boyhood and a faithful churchwarden until the end of his days.

In his address on this occasion the Rt Rev Percy Herbert, Bishop

Sidney Grapes was a chorister and churchwarden at Potter Heigham church

of Norwich, said: 'It is not given to many writers to create fictitious characters that are so alive, and that once met with will never be forgotten . . . he made them living people, each with their own special character, but each the kind of people that we felt we'd known all our lives. He takes his place in that sense with the immortal characters invented by Charles Dickens . . . he was not only an astonishingly fine natural humorist, he was an incomparable teller of good stories.'

That sort of praise has echoed across the decades for a Norfolk rustic comedian, garage proprietor and man of letters with the evergreen touch.

11

Tom Higdon (1869–1939) and Kitty Higdon (1864–1946)

Teachers who began the Burston School Strike

'Pupil power' in a small and scattered south Norfolk hamlet fashioned the longest strike recorded in English history. The Burston School Strike, started by children when their teachers were dismissed in April 1914, went on until just before the outbreak of the Second World War. It stands among the most stirring examples of common people in adversity squaring up to authority.

Teachers Tom and Kitty Higdon arrived in Burston in 1911, a married couple, Christian Socialists, both of an independent turn of mind and long associated with extra-curricular activities in helping to organise the agricultural workers. Tom Higdon was born in 1869, son of a Somerset labourer. His wife was five years older. They met while teaching in London and moved to Norfolk at the turn of the century to take a post at Wood Dalling, a small community a few miles west of Aylsham. It was here they first encountered trouble with school managers – trouble that led to their transfer to Burston. It followed them there.

Tom Higdon wrote about what they found on arrival in Burston: 'Landlord, parson and farmer held sway over the area in many respects more completely than in the district left behind. Parson and farmer ruled the Burston Parish Council. Housing conditions were extremely bad, overcrowding occurring seriously. The school premises were ill-lighted, ill-drained, badly-heated and wretchedly ventilated. Thus there was much radical wrong, which for very conscience sake, as well as for all practical and healthful reasons, must needs be faced.'

TOM HIGDON AND KITTY HIGDON

Tom and Kitty Higdon

Tom and Kitty soon met fierce opposition from the Vicar, the Rev Charles Tucker Eland, chairman of the school governors, self-appointed upholder of the social and economic status quo and a bigot who expected total deference from his flock. But the Higdons couldn't change. Tom went on organising new branches of the Agricultural Labourers' Union and led the labourers in a take-over of the parish council. Kitty kept on speaking her mind at managers' meetings. The children loved their teachers and so did most of the parents.

A crisis flared up early in 1914 when the vicar charged the Higdons with unjustly caning two Barnardo children. There was an inquiry by the Norfolk Education Committee. The charge remained unproven but then other matters were brought up – and the Higdons were dismissed. However, neither parents nor children would accept the decision and a series of indignant meetings were held on Burston Green. All but a few of the pupils went on strike, supported by their parents. Fines were doled out for non-attendance, but the money to pay them was raised at gatherings attended by increasing numbers of supporters from the surrounding countryside.

The Agricultural Labourers' Union and the National Union of Railwaymen rallied to the strikers' cause, and their anger increased when Burston villagers supporting the teachers were deprived of their glebe land by the vicar. Support for the pro-Higdon minority on the executive of the National Union of Teachers grew. Campaign meetings were held over a wide area of Norfolk, and a series of London gatherings organised by the NUR saw the Higdons and some of their striking pupils and parents appearing on the platform. Funds were raised all over the country and money even came from abroad. A new school was built in 1917 on the edge of Burston Green and opened with great enthusiasm.

The strike had started in April 1914, just a few months before the outbreak of hostilities in Europe, but the remarkable loyalty to the teachers in Burston and the passionate indignation it inspired all over the county did not cool, and working people continued the fight against rural injustice at home throughout the war.

The Burston Strike School prospered throughout the 1920s, when senior children were taken to trade union meetings as part of their education and as an expression of the unity of the school with the struggles of the exploited. Meetings in the school, 'a centre of rural democracy', were held in support of the Russian Revolution and for Russian famine relief and land restoration. The school went on until Tom Higdon died in 1939 on the eve of the Second World War. Kitty then went into sad decline, and several times was found wandering the lanes at night, saying she was waiting for him to return home from a union meeting. She died in 1946.

TOM HIGDON AND KITTY HIGDON

They rest side by side in the churchyard of the village they brought to national prominence and served so well. Hard by, the Strike School building stands on the edge of the Green, now a meeting place and memorial to a genuine expression of grass-roots democracy. There's an annual march and celebration with speeches by socialist leaders and prominent trade unionists.

In *The Burston Rebellion*, Tom Higdon wrote: 'Some of the most beautiful things in this struggle have been the wonderful endurance, self-sacrifice and devotion of the parents who, from their own small share and at considerable expense to themselves, especially during the first year of the strike, brought vegetables, bread, eggs, cakes, confections, furniture and books for the school etc, thus sparing expense to the teachers in order that they might be able to hold out longer. Latterly the letters and

The Strike School stands at the edge of the Green at Burston

subscriptions of supporting comrades in other parts of the country has been a source of deep inspiration and great encouragement.'

It was the children themselves, however, who had turned deep grievances into open rebellion after a protest meeting on the village green. Violet Potter and another senior girl chalked 'We are going on strike tomorrow' on the schoolroom blackboard so it would be seen when put up on the easel the next day. A similar announcement on a slate was hung up in the porch, while the village signpost and several gates were chalked with the same words.

By the time the school was due to open on 1st April 1914, the Green was crowded with children being shepherded into a procession by Violet Potter and her helpers, senior pupils and parents, and their names checked with the list. When the supply teacher arrived to take over from the Higdons as the school bell rang out, the procession moved off. Children waved little red flags and Union Jacks, marching to the music of Violet Potter on the concertina. Some carried large cards aloft with the slogans: 'We want our teachers back' and 'Justice we want'. At the head of the procession was a banner loaned by the woman who kept the village shop. It was inscribed with just one word – 'Justice'.

The longest strike in English history was underway in a little Norfolk village in the name of two well-loved teachers who simply refused to yield to petty local tyranny.

12

Robert Kett (1492–1549)

Rebel Leader of the Norfolk Peasantry

It took 400 years for Robert Kett to be transformed from traitor and murderer to freedom fighter and hero.

In 1549 this member of Norfolk's lesser gentry was hanged for leading a rebellion against his legally appointed monarch and the social order of the day. In 1949 a large stone plaque was fixed on the wall of Norwich Castle. It was placed there by 'the citizens of Norwich in reparation and honour to a notable and courageous leader in the long struggle of the common people of England to escape from a servile life into the freedom of just conditions.'

Kett was 57, a tanner by trade and a landowner in Wymondham, when he became the people's champion and spearheaded an uprising that would lead to the deaths of over 3,000 of his followers. This is primarily an East Anglian drama although its roots lie buried deep within social and political events of 16th century England as a whole. The country was in religious and economic turmoil. There was much raising of rents, but the biggest concern was over the enclosure of common land by the local gentry, which threatened the livelihoods of the peasants. There had been widespread disorder and rioting in many counties in 1549 but it was only in Norfolk that the peasantry found a leader of outstanding quality. Although a landowner himself, Kett was obviously moved by the plight of the rioters. Perhaps his religious convictions and sense of moral outrage at the way the commoners were being treated persuaded him to fall in with the rioters. Certainly his exceptional talents for leadership helped transform a disorderly mob into a great demonstrating force.

Robert Kett strove to make clear he was not rebelling against the government in London but seeking to reform local government in Norfolk. His petition to the young king Edward VI was politely phrased and throughout the whole uprising he acted with restraint and moderation. He made an indelible impression on the Norfolk of his day, dominating affairs of the county for six weeks. Establishing an orderly camp on Mousehold Heath overlooking Norwich, he was joined by almost 20,000 men.

Edward's protector, the Duke of Somerset, sent the Royal Herald from London and offered a pardon to followers of the 'Captain of Mischief' though his accompanying sword bearer was unable to arrest Kett because of a large number of faithful supporters around him.

The Herald withdrew to report back to Somerset. Kett led a successful attack on Norwich and his followers took over the city. They defeated a force sent by Somerset and led by the Marquess of Northampton. However, there was to be no ultimate denial of the forces of the government.

Somerset quickly gathered together a much larger army of some 10,000 men who marched upon Norwich. They were led by John Dudley, at that time Earl of Warwick. Dudley's troops cut Kett's supply lines, stormed the city, and finally routed the core of Kett's peasant army at the Battle of Dussindale.

About 3,000 rebels perished in the battle, sited in a low valley just north of Norwich and now a large housing development. The aftermath was as horrible as might be expected at that time. The rebels, who had rejected repeated offers of pardon, were guilty of treason under the law and the penalty prescribed was death. Nine of their leaders were hanged, drawn and quartered on Mousehold Heath. Others died on gallows outside the Magdalen Gate and 300 were said to have been hanged in the market place.

Kett himself fled the battlefield where trained soldiers easily crushed the peasants. He rode alone for about ten miles to the

Robert Kett sitting under the Oak of Reformation (Ashburton's History of England, 1793)

village of Swannington where he was recognised, seized and handed over to the authorities in Norwich. With his brother William, also captured after the battle, he was sent to London and imprisoned in the Tower while awaiting trial. Both were condemned to death and taken back to Norfolk for execution. William Kett was hanged from the tall west tower of Wymondham Abbey. In Norwich, Robert Kett was taken from his cell in the Guildhall to the castle and hanged in chains from the battlements.

Kett's rebellion was the most serious of civil disturbances in England during that turbulent year and it helped bring about the fall of the Duke of Somerset's protectorate. The Duke himself was executed three years later for plotting against his successor, the same John Dudley who had defeated Kett and who became Duke of Northumberland.

The rebellion, while arousing mixed emotions in Norfolk at the time, became a tragic legend, reinforcing the East Anglian's suspicions of outside interference, whether by legislation or military force. Kett eventually was to be hailed a Norfolk hero, an embodiment of resolute independence. The story handed down for generations reflected the Norfolkman's idea of his own ideals and attitudes and the stand he was willing to make when these were challenged.

Of course, many questions still linger over Robert Kett's role in one of the bloodiest sagas the region has ever witnessed. Would riot have turned into rebellion had he refused to join the rioters from the outset? Perhaps, lacking a leader, the disgruntled commoners would have returned home and continued to quietly nurse their grievances. The sudden and brutal ending of Kett's rebellion left deep wounds that would take many generations to heal. The betrayal, as many rebels saw it, of a popular movement concerned only with justice and good government by the bureaucratic London authorities was simply another pointer towards the unfairness of an unjust rule. The very fact that the government felt compelled to react so harshly towards the rebels was taken by many as a clear indication of the reasonable nature of rebel claims. The local governing class, to which Robert Kett might easily have aspired, was mainly corrupt and, supported by higher ranks in society, succeeded in exploiting its position and the relative weakness of the poorer classes that made up the bulk of country dwellers.

Kett's reply to the words of the Royal Herald on Mousehold

Heath before the attack on Norwich offers some measure of his character: 'Kings and princes are wont to pardon wicked persons, not innocent and just ones. We, for our part, have deserved nothing and are guilty to ourselves of no crime, and therefore we despise such speeches as idle and unprofitable to our business. I trust I have done nothing but what belongs to the duty of a true subject.'

Kett's Oak, to be found on the A11 road between Wymondham and Hethersett, is reputed to be the tree under which Kett and his followers assembled before they set off for Norwich. According to the chroniclers, Kett issued a strong rallying call here. Whether the tree, marked and railed off, was actually chosen by Kett remains open to question. However, it symbolises the emergence of a leader of the 'poor commoners'.

13

Jem Mace (1831–1910)

King of the Ring

Ever since I discovered that Jem Mace, father of modern scientific boxing, had the good fortune to be born in the same mid-Norfolk village as me it's been 'second's out' for another round of praise.

As soon as the art of name-dropping meant a place in grown-up conversations, I told anyone who would listen that a very famous sportsman came from my home patch at Beeston. If they simply shrugged or didn't seem too impressed I'd reel off facts and figures culled from a book where I'd been properly introduced to my first sporting hero. Unabashed by adult apathy I continued to spread the Mace gospel. It was a cause of great pride when Beeston's most famous son was suitably honoured by the unveiling of a memorial in the village churchyard in 1976.

Born on 8th April 1831, son of the village blacksmith, Jem soon developed into 'a merry handful' and resisted all attempts to put him into the same trade as his father and the three other Mace boys. He was eventually packed off to Wells-next-the-Sea to learn the trade of a cabinet-maker, but spent most of his time playing the fiddle 'like an angel'. His master, a publican, kept him entertaining customers rather than learning about making cabinets. Jem decided to travel around the country, attending shows, fairs and village inns, seeking work with his fiddle – and later with his fists. He'd already shown plenty of promise as a pugilist in his native village where local girls were apt to bestow favours on boys most willing to prove their superiority in 'needle' fights. Though Mace probably got involved in such fights due

JEM MACE (1831–1910)

Jem Mace

more to a natural inclination for the game rather than to impress the young ladies.

Mace was 18, around 11 stone, and beautifully proportioned when an episode in Yarmouth pointed to his future destiny. He was playing his fiddle in the streets when three rough young fishermen accosted him, knocking the beloved instrument from his hand and smashing it. Jem challenged and defeated two of the assailants while the third took to his heels. An appreciative crowd took up a collection and one man, subscribing a guinea, said that a chap who was as useful as that with his fists really ought to be a prizefighter . . .

Jem fashioned his trade in the boxing booths, fearlessly taking on all comers, but preferring to use gloves rather than fighting with his bare fists. He was called the Swaffham Gypsy, although it is unlikely he had any Romany blood. Early successes brought him to the attention of Nat Langham, a popular figure in the fight game, who was keen to match him with Bill Thorpe, a clever middleweight. Jem's strict training routine saw him rise at dawn and take a warm bath, followed by a vigorous rubbing with coarse towels and brushes. Next, a trot of about ten miles well muffled in sweaters. This distance would be gradually increased until the fighter could easily cope with ten miles out and ten miles back at a sharp pace. In training for bare-fist bouts, the hands and face were often pickled in a mixture of various ingredients until the skin was almost as hard as leather.

Mace met Thorpe in February 1857 in Kent. The amount of interest aroused could be gauged by Nat Langham's whisper to Jem as he entered the ring: 'Mind you win, lad, there's more than £2,000 on you.' Mace outclassed and badly punished the plucky Thorpe and won in the 17th round. Within four years he was battling for the heavyweight championship of England against the title-holder Sam Hurst, who also happened to be champion wrestler of Lancashire. Mace proved too strong for his giant opponent and Hurst's beating was so severe that his life was in danger for three days. Happily, he rallied and made a good recovery.

Mace defended his crown against Tom King the following January and came out victorious after 43 rounds of fierce combat. King, however, won a return match and then, after beating American champion John Heenan for the world title, decided to retire. So Mace took over and became universally known as world champion after beating Joe Goss of Wolverhampton on 1st September 1863 in one hour and 44 minutes.

A year later, the Norfolk man accepted the challenge of Joe Coburn, the American champion, but when Coburn insisted that the bout must be refereed by a personal friend it was called off. Coburn returned to America and Mace didn't fight again until May 1866 when he again went in the ring against Joe Goss. It ended in a draw. Goss was offered one more chance – and this time Mace trounced him in 21 rounds.

At this time public revulsion against prizefighting, led by the clergy, swept the country. Staging bouts became a tricky business. Mace, matched with Baldwin, the Irish Giant, was arrested on the eve of battle and bound over to keep the peace. Seeing no prospect of further fights at home, Mace set sail for America where boxing was booming. He was soon paired with Tom Allen, who laid claim to the American championship. The purse was £2,000 and the championship of the world at stake. They clashed in New Orleans. Allen was outclassed from the start but fought on gamely for 44 rounds. When at last he was led away confessing defeat, Allen had a dislocated jaw and shoulder. He was 26, Mace 39.

Mace tried to get a square fight with Joe Coburn. When they did meet, however, a referee in fear of his life was only too willing to call it a draw. Mace retired soon after but continued to box in exhibitions. His friends in New York presented him with a fine

The memorial to Jem Mace in Beeston churchyard

silver belt, which now resides in The Ring Museum in Madison Square Garden in New York City.

In his later years Mace became landlord of the Swan pub in Norwich. He died in Liverpool on 10th November 1910. A white stone memorial to him, which had been moved around Norwich Cemetery and then lodged for several years in a city stonemason's yard, was retrieved and transferred to his home village. Proudly inscribed 'Jem Mace, Champion of the World' and placed here by 'a few of his old friends', it underlines Beeston's pride in the blacksmith's son who forged an international reputation by bringing a peerless science to a tough but noble sport. A corner in the village pub, the Ploughshare, is dedicated to Mace's exploits and displays many photographs and cuttings – bringing new meaning to the old cry of 'get a round in'.

14

Mary Mann (1848–1929)

Chronicler of the Victorian Countryside

Hailed as Norfolk's answer to Thomas Hardy and much admired by the young D.H. Lawrence, Mary Mann, a farmer's wife, produced superbly-crafted stories packed with acute feeling for rich dialect and ruined lives. Reviewing her novel *The Parish Nurse* in 1905, Hugh Massingham wrote: 'Norfolk has in her a writer of whom it may well be proud, who should in time come into her kingdom.'

Sadly, that expectation has not been realised. Mary Mann still waits for the full recognition she deserves for gritty work shedding light on the hardship of life in the Victorian countryside. She was determined to show rural plight rather than rustic charm in her writing. Her most celebrated stories, first published in 1902, are contained in *The Fields of Dulditch*, which offers brutal accounts of the lives of labouring families at a time when demeaning poverty was not only commonplace but seemingly inevitable.

A merchant's daughter and born in Norwich, Mary married a local squire, Mr Fairman Mann in 1871 and moved to the small village of Shropham, near Attleborough, first to Church Farm and then to her husband's family seat at Shropham Manor. The shock of leaving a bustling city for a country backwater was compounded by the onset of an agricultural depression that wrecked livelihoods across Norfolk. At a time when foot-and-mouth was considered a minor and wholly treatable condition, it was anthrax that was the killer. Then there were plummeting prices caused by a flood of cheap grain from the New World.

MARY MANN (1848–1929)

Mary Mann

Mary saw the effects locally in overgrown fields, derelict farms and blighted hopes. Here she produced a series of five novels and four outstanding volumes of short stories, drawing heavily on the sufferings and injustices of the area and marked by a bitter humour. The harrowing tales in *The Fields of Dulditch*, in particular, stand as the perfect answer to any nostalgic visions we may still harbour about the 'good old days' on the land at the turn of the last century. In an unpublished foreword to this book, Mary describes that fictional village, based on Shropham, as 'a depressing neighbourhood, certainly. As I detail its several features I am appalled at the bleakness, the dreariness of the prospect.'

Brutal truth was the clear object in her rural tales. *Ben Pitcher's Elly* deals candidly with a woman who murders her illegitimate child. The anti-hero of *Wolf Charlie* takes his name 'by reason of the famished look in his melancholy eyes, of the way in which the skin of his lips drawn tightly over his gums exposes his great yellow teeth; by reason of the leanness of his flanks, the shaggy, unkempt hair about his head and face, the half fierce, half frightened expression.' This impoverished stone-breaker acquires an instant family in the form of a deserted wife with one leg and five children.

Perhaps the grimmest episode of all from another stark series is *Little Brother*, where the thirteenth child of a farm labourer's wife is stillborn. A charitable spinster, arriving to console the mother, finds the body missing from the cot and the children downstairs playing with what seems to be a battered doll. Chided for allowing such desecration, the mother replies: 'Other folke's child'en have a toy, now and then, to cape 'em out o' mischief. My little'uns han't. He've kep'em quiet for hours, the po'r baby have, and I'll lay a crown they han't done no harm to their little brother.'

Including this saga in her selection for *The Oxford Book of English*

Stories, A.S. Byatt describes it as 'plain and brief, and clear and terrible . . . she is recording, not judging, but her telling is spiky with morals and the inadequacy of morals.' Norwich-raised novelist and biographer D.J. Taylor, one of Mary Mann's main champions in recent years, says: 'The best of the Dulditch tales are unlike anything else in Victorian literature – hard-eyed, sympathetic, direct, unyielding.'

While Fairman Mann farmed 800 acres and assumed the role of caring squire, Mary helped teach reading at the village school, organised treats and was a frequent visitor to the labourers' homes. When her husband died in 1913, she took a home at Winterton and finally moved to Sheringham on the North Norfolk coast. In that unpublished foreword to the Dulditch stories, Mary described her husband as 'a man, well-to-do, kind and generous once; an excellent husband, father (one son, three daughters), master, farmer; getting now poor in pocket, shorter in temper; year by year, a man who has struggled in a dogged, quiet fashion, but who is beaten and knows it, finding the knowledge bitter to a degree . . .'

Mary Mann's gravestone in Shropham churchyard, now split and crumbling, is an open book. The barely legible epitaph reads: 'We bring our years to an end as it were a tale that is told.'

When *The Fields of Dulditch* was republished in 1976, sparking new hopes of belated but genuine appreciation of her work, Ronald Blythe said in his introduction: 'Although she reproduces the picturesque speech patterns of this lowly, grimly-rooted and – for her – blighted society with sufficient colour to entertain the reader, her central purpose is not to show rustic charm but rural plight. By enduring the misfortune of their birth, their ignorance, their incessant toil and their malnutrition, her characters receive their own special nobility, and it is this which ultimately concerns her. She describes first the barren soil of a particular life and then the little miracle of its flowering.'

Adrian Bell, arguably the finest writer on country matters to light up the furrows of East Anglia, said memorably: 'The people of Dulditch are more real to me than Hardy's . . . although the record of rural penury is so shocking that it awes the writing to simplicity, it leaves an epic quality in the mind, a sort of noble rage which makes for life.'

15

Sarah Martin (1791–1843)

The Angel of The Bridewell

Mention Norfolk women and prison reform, and most observations will begin and end with the outstanding work of Elizabeth Fry. But a thin little figure in black dress and bonnet, both old and carefully mended, deserves much more than a passing nod in recognition of her lifetime of offering help and hope to those who needed it most in Yarmouth Infirmary, the Workhouse and The Bridewell.

These were all on the same grim site facing the Market Place when Sarah Martin, a Sunday School teacher at the parish church, took her first steps in 1810 on a long and difficult journey that was inspired by a warm heart and dauntless spirit. When her work took her to Yarmouth, Sarah began making visits to the Workhouse and Infirmary where she chatted and read to sick and aged inmates and instructed children in the Scriptures. Prison visiting had been her main desire from an early age, but it wasn't until August 1818 that she was able to inch her way into what had been hitherto strictly forbidden territory.

Sarah had seen wretched vagabonds and short-term prisoners brought into The Bridewell, often bleeding after being flogged at the Market Cross. She initially talked her way in to see a woman who had brutally ill-treated her child – and she did not let the door close against her again. She went regularly to read the Bible to prisoners, who relished this sudden interest shown in them. She kept exact records of each inmate, including name, age, sentence, whether able to read and write when coming into prison and what their attainments were on leaving.

Sarah was an exceptionally gifted teacher and it is remarkable how many learned to read while they were there. Her first efforts to find useful occupations for prisoners were inspired by her own training as a dressmaker – she decided to show the women how to sew. When garments were sold she put a small sum aside for the workers so that when they were released they would have enough to buy a new dress and perhaps keep them while looking for employment. The men were taught to sew as well, making caps and mending their threadbare clothes.

Sarah kept a journal and its entries underline the value of these lessons: 'Bevington had begged me for some pieces of cloth to mend his trousers. He had them and they are done extremely well. His appearance is much more respectable with clothing well mended. Bailey begged of me a piece to mend his blue slop. I gave it him and it is done very well.' Sarah collected bones from the kitchens of her friends and set the men to work carving out spoons, buttons and seals. These she sold and kept the money for when the men were discharged.

Her heart seemed to be given most readily to young boys in prison and at one time she took a group of five under her wing, reading illustrated books to them as a reward for good behaviour. She provides a touching account of the way they crowded round, sizing up the pictures, and begging her to leave them until the next day so they could look again. They were eager to please but couldn't refrain from quarrelling and she often arrived to find one of them put in the cell. She then suggested a set of rules to which they should sign their names or make their mark. If they kept them they should each have a grey cotton shirt to go out with when discharged. Rules drawn up included:

- To try to become better boys before we leave the jail.
- To leave off quarrelling and fighting and swearing and stealing one another's victuals.

- Instead of being always finding fault with the other four – to be quiet and find fault with myself.
- To mind what the Governor says – and not compel him to put me in the cell.

Sarah also carried out many good works for the poor and destitute outside prison, in the town. This began after the attempted suicide of a young woman, Hannah Page, who tried to hang herself but was found just in time. Sarah immediately launched a fund for 'Employment for the Destitute', which provided work for female prisoners on discharge or help for prisoners' wives, or for anyone else in real need who fell outside the scope of Poor Law provisions. Various items in her accounts book show the range of help given: a donkey was found for one man, lodgings were paid for another, a woman was paid to attend a confinement instead of a doctor. There were gifts of flour and yeast and some were helped to redeem clothing from the pawnshop. Sarah also regarded books and writing materials for her pupils as necessities.

There were occasional attempts to persuade her to accept payment from the Corporation, but she refused on the grounds that if she were a paid employee, prisoners would regard her as part of the establishment and respond less readily. However, her health, never particularly robust, began to fail in the spring of 1841 and the Jail Committee recommended that she should be allowed twelve pounds a year. Sarah repeated her objections to being paid, only to be told very firmly that if she did not accept the offer her visits to the jail would be forbidden.

Her back pains grew worse and she was given morphine to relieve them. She died on 15th October 1843 and was buried near her grandmother in Caister churchyard, not far from the town she served so well. Her tombstone is on the left of the church door. Sarah's parents had died when she was young and

Sarah Martin's grave in Caister churchyard

she was raised by her grandmother, Mrs Bonnet, a glove maker who lived in a small thatched cottage on Beach Road in Caister. The Beach Road cottage is still there and in good shape.

Apart from a few bequests, Sarah's meagre possessions were left to the British and Foreign Bible Society. Her death created a stir in the national newspapers and a window was dedicated to her memory in Yarmouth's parish church of St Nicholas. This was destroyed by bombing during the Second World War, but when the church was rebuilt in 1961 a panel in the west window featured Sarah Martin ministering to prisoners.

It was a bishop, giving a donation to the memorial window fund in 1843, who said: 'I would canonise Sarah Martin if I could.'

16

Harriet Martineau (1802–1876)

Queen of Journalism

One of Norfolk's most distinguished literary daughters also scored remarkable personal victories over physical disabilities, poverty and misfortune. From a Cinderella-type existence – she was born without the sensations of taste and smell and her hearing began to go at the age of twelve – Harriet Martineau blossomed into the nation's Queen of Journalism. She made it possible for women to fill more exalted positions and do nobler work than before, while every movement that had for its aim the well-being of the masses found in her a staunch supporter.

Harriet sought her early refuge in religion and books after discovering *Paradise Lost* at the age of seven. Shy, plain and sensitive, the sixth of the eight children of Norwich bombazine manufacturer Thomas Martineau and his wife Elizabeth, she was born in Gurney Court, off Magdalen Street in Norwich. This had also been the birthplace of social reformer Elizabeth Fry in 1780. The Martineau family then moved into No. 24 Magdalen Street – 'a handsome, plain brick house . . . prosaic to the last degree' is how Harriet described it. She was raised in a stern and resolutely pious atmosphere. Hopes of becoming a teacher were shattered by increasing deafness, and so she turned to writing. Her mother felt she would be better employed in sewing, but Harriet began to write anonymously for the *Monthly Repository*, a Unitarian periodical.

In 1826 her father's business crashed and the shock killed him. Harriet had become engaged, but her fiancé, a Manchester

HARRIET MARTINEAU (1802–1876)

Harriet Martineau

minister, died from a brain illness around the same time. Thus, freed from the restrictions on her life that a Victorian marriage would have imposed upon her, and by now acutely aware of the inequalities and miseries of her fellows, she set out on a lifelong study of social reform, politics and economics. Her ability in the latter two became the golden coach that conveyed her to a celebrity's life in London. Her first book, *Illustrations of Political Economy*, was published in 1832 with the help of Charles Fox and brought immediate success, including financial independence.

Harriet saw herself as a national educator and produced hundreds of articles, leaders, pamphlets, reviews and over 40 major works. Captivated by the Lake District, in 1845 she built a home in Ambleside for life. While not immortalising the district in the same way as her neighbour Wordsworth, she penned a comprehensive guide to the area. From her home, The Knoll, she lectured to local labourers, founded a building society to benefit 15 families and continued her philanthropic rounds.

She lived modestly, occasionally frugally. In 1840 during an illness that ended in a controversial mesmeric cure, friends raised a testimonial fund of £14,000. But if money was short, literary fame increased. George Eliot said Miss Martineau was the only Englishwoman to possess thoroughly the art of writing, and Harriet's novel *Deerbrook* received Charlotte Brontë's congratulations. The French philosopher and social theorist Auguste Comte surprisingly preferred his disciples to read Harriet's condensed version of the *Philosophie Positive*, financed by a former High Sheriff of Norfolk, rather than his original. Praise indeed!

Her rapier-pen, exposing evils, created the first great female impact and was made without male patronage or legislation. She supported mining and public health legislation; defended the Co-operative movement, the Chartists and Friendly Societies; fought the unhealthy window tax, unjust indirect tax and faulty patent and copyright laws. She wrote passionately against the huge number of offences punishable by death, the retributive prison system, cruelties of the press gang, patronage in public service and treatment of the insane. Vocally, she acclaimed land reforms, better housing and a fair wage. Her book *Society in America*, stated by Charles Dickens to be the best ever written on that country, followed an extensive two-year fact-finding mission which even threats of lynching could not curtail. There was a public outcry when she supported philosophic atheism, claiming theology lacked scientific proof. Although a far cry from Octagon Chapel days in Norwich, when she won all three prizes in a national Unitarian essay competition, she was testifying, as usual, to truth as she saw it. Credibility unimpaired, Harriet's finest hour came a year later.

In 1852 she became the first woman leader writer on a London newspaper, the highly-respected *Daily News*. At first submitting two leaders a week, she soon became responsible for all six. She provided 1,642 excellent leaders, each taking less than three hours to compose, over 14 gratifying years until forced to resign through ill-health. She missed just one deadline – when her niece forgot to post the copy. Meanwhile articles flowed to numerous periodicals on every conceivable subject.

Harriet Martineau obviously possessed infinite knowledge and masterly appreciation of contemporary events and opinions and an outstanding flair for journalism. Despite a society prejudiced against women writers, she expounded daily to the nation on domestic and international affairs. In her influential position she led the public in their views, not least regarding major conflicts. As well as ranting at government inefficiencies and publicising Florence Nightingale's proposed army reform during the Crimean War, her far-sighted solution to India's problems, accelerated by the mutiny, foreshadowed British policy by nearly 100 years. Her American connections rendered the *Daily News* unrivalled in disclosures on the civil war despite its obvious Northern bias.

This pioneer female traveller became an invalid from 1855 and never again visited her native county, although she had been back two years earlier to enjoy a happy holiday at Cromer. The Queen of Journalism died on 27th June 1876, receiving a simple burial in the family plot at Birmingham's Key Hill cemetery, and an unadorned tombstone bearing her name, age and places of birth and death. Harriet Martineau might not have received her rightful place in posterity, but her autobiography shows she cared little for that: 'Of posthumous fame I have not the slightest expectation or desire. To be useful in my day and generation is enough for me.'

However, these words in a review of her book in the *Athenaeum Magazine* of 1849 do epitomise her achievements: 'She has spared no pains in investigating the truth and allowed no fears to prevent her from stating it.'

17

Kenneth McKee (1906–1990)

Pioneer of Hip Replacements

Kenneth McKee was a pioneering surgeon who made the lame walk again. But he had to cope with immense medical scepticism before evidence of his remarkable work became too overwhelming to ignore. Appointed Registrar at the Norfolk & Norwich Hospital in 1932, Ken McKee developed one of modern medicine's most successful operations – the hip replacement.

Orthopaedic surgery proved a fertile field for a man fascinated by all things mechanical. A youthful interest in taking motorcycles and cars to pieces helped to prepare him for an outstandingly inventive career. There was scant backing from the medical establishment, but exciting success arrived when he used a cobalt-chrome alloy for the ball-and-socket joint, which he developed with the help of his senior Registrar, John Watson-Farrar. McKee demonstrated his first cases at Cambridge in 1951 and later at the Royal Society of Medicine in 1957. He and Watson-Farrar jointly published a classic paper on the subject in 1966. But, as McKee himself recorded, he 'came under considerable criticism and was looked upon with disapproval'.

McKee and Sir John Charnley of Manchester were the chief pioneers of total hip replacement, one of the great advances in surgery of the 20th century. The Norwich surgeon persevered with his work while Charnley was still pessimistic about the outcome of this type of operation. The key to early success was cobalt-chrome, a metal that proved particularly suitable for use as an artificial joint. 'I used to take my motorbike to pieces and

Kenneth McKee

put it back together again and do a lot on the car. And when you have a joint go on a car, the obvious thing is to replace it,' was the straightforward McKee formula. He also developed replacement joints for knees and elbows and clamps for treating leg fractures. One of his patients, a retired accountant who had both hips replaced at the same time, later became a golfing partner.

When the revolutionary concept began to gain acceptance among the medical profession, top surgeons from all over the world came to Norwich to learn about the technique. By the time he retired in 1971, McKee had replaced over a thousand hips. Today about 50,000 hips are replaced each year in the United Kingdom.

KENNETH MCKEE (1906–1990)

In his day a keen sailor, skier and golfer, Ken McKee was also a committed Christian. For his work he was rewarded with a CBE in 1972, and an Honorary Doctorate of Science from Cambridge University three years later. He was awarded the Honorary Fellowship of the Royal Society of Medicine in 1986. High standards have been maintained by successors in the orthopaedic department of the Norfolk & Norwich Hospital, and similar departments have since been established at the Queen Elizabeth Hospital at King's Lynn and the James Paget Hospital, Gorleston.

When I conducted a Poll of the Century in the *Eastern Daily Press* in 1999, McKee was voted by readers as Norfolk's most influential figure of the 20th century. He led the way by a clear margin from naturalist Ted Ellis, lifeboatman Henry Blogg and nurse Edith Cavell. McKee's widow Dan, said at the time that she had derived great pleasure and pride from the results of the poll. 'He was a very modest man. He never sought fame, only recognition and encouragement for his inventions. It is wonderful to know so many people are still being helped by his work.'

Among numerous glowing testimonies to the work of this surgeon came this one from Betty Richardson of Sheringham: 'He saved my life in 1948. I was nursing at the Norfolk & Norwich Hospital and he found I had a serious spinal condition. He got me into hospital within a week and I was put straight onto a plaster bed. Mr McKee operated a week later, grafting my lumbar spine with a graft from my iliac crest. I was on a plaster bed for three months. He carried out an amazing operation which has allowed me to be mobile ever since.

'He did a second spinal fusion about 12 years later. I certainly owe my life and mobility to him. People always associate him with hip surgery, but he was a brilliant orthopaedic surgeon and engineer in many other ways.'

Hilton Edwards of Gorleston recalled the debt he owed to Ken McKee and fellow surgeon John Watson-Farrar. 'They operated on me in 1960 after a bad motorbike accident. One of my legs was so shattered it had to be put together like a jigsaw puzzle with plates, screws and pins. The operation was such a success that I was able to resume heavy work until my retirement.'

There were many other tributes from hip replacement patients – and from a surgeon who started performing the procedure only four years after McKee's first published paper. Hugh Phillips was then a junior surgeon at the Norfolk & Norwich Hospital. Since then he has seen countless changes and improvements in the operation. But few of them have gathered as much interest as the latest developments in keyhole surgery.

Mr Phillips, now consultant orthopaedic surgeon at the new Norfolk & Norwich Hospital at Colney on the outskirts of the city, and vice president of the College of Surgeons, said that McKee and Watson-Farrar would have been delighted that their work had progressed so far. For developers of the 'two-incision technique' were claiming it could allow patients to go home the day after they had a hip replacement as opposed to the average eight-day hospital stay that was previously necessary. This could cut waiting lists and save the NHS millions of pounds.

In the operation, the replacement joint is inserted through two cuts as small as 4 to 5 cms long. Muscles are moved aside. The traditional procedure had required a 30 cm incision and extensive cutting of the leg and hip muscles. Benefits of the new technique include shorter hospital stays, smaller scars, reduced blood loss, faster and less painful rehabilitation and the chance of a quicker return to daily life.

Mr Phillips said that this would not have happened without the determination, courage and intellect of Ken McKee. 'He was a true visionary. He was met with a lot of scepticism, some detractors thought he was mad, but he saw the light and stuck to what he believed.'

18

Horatio Nelson (1758–1805)

From Burnham Thorpe to Trafalgar

The boy from Burnham Thorpe who became the first truly popular British hero continues to provoke fierce debate over his life and achievements.

Struck down at the moment of his greatest triumph during the Battle of Trafalgar in 1805, Horatio Nelson was recognised even in his own time as the greatest naval tactician the country had produced. A born leader, he inspired his men to remarkable heights. Set against this were personal traits which were the despair of his friends and provided ready ammunition for his detractors. His notorious affair with Emma Hamilton and estrangement from a loyal wife were the talk of the country and undoubtedly led to his exclusion from sections of the establishment and society.

Nelson was excessively vain, his general stance and flaunting of awards and decorations going well beyond a justifiable pride in his own achievements. Still, it is this potent combination of brave, talented commander and vain, naïve lover that has made the Norfolk man such an enigmatic character, able to attract the attention of people from all walks of life over the centuries.

Nelson was a true product of his environment. He was a Norfolkman in his independence of mind and distrust of foreigners. He numbered more than a dozen parsons among his relatives and immediate forebears and would have possessed a strong sense of spiritual privilege and self confidence. His mother's death when he was nine left him to the mercies of village women when he was not away at school at Norwich or

Horatio Nelson

North Walsham. His liking for them and sympathy for the poverty of their families gave him an understanding of farm labourers and, later, of seamen that became part of the secret of his brilliance as a commander. Nelson was loved by his men. Visiting wounded sailors in hospital at Yarmouth after the Battle of Copenhagen he noticed a young man who, like himself, had lost his right arm. 'Why, Jack,' he exclaimed, 'you and I are spoiled for fishermen.'

Nelson took with him to sea several Norfolk boys as 'captain's servants' to be trained as officers. Among them were the sons of the rectors of Rollesby (Billy Bolton), Sedgeford (Thomas Weatherhead) and Tittleshall (William Hoste). His own servant Tom Allen was one of the men he enlisted from the Burnhams to serve as a seaman, and he proved a true Norfolkman – when King Ferdinand came aboard the flagship at Naples and extended a hand to be kissed, Allen shook it and said in a broad Norfolk accent: 'How d'yer dew, Mr King!'

Nelson insisted that he gloried in being a Norfolk native and spoke of 'dear, dear Burnham', associating it with the happy days of childhood before the death of his mother. 'The thought of former days brings all my mother to my heart, which shows itself in my eyes.' He never returned to Burnham Thorpe after his recall to sea in February 1793, even for his father's funeral there – because he feared he might bump into his estranged wife at the graveside. So his only visits were to Yarmouth but Norfolk in general kept in touch with him and his mounting fame. His victories were celebrated with parades, dinners and dances, and pubs were named after him. To this day, on the anniversary of his death at Trafalgar on 21st October 1805, the church of All Saints at Burnham Thorpe, where his father was rector, flies from its tower a replica of the flag he flew at the Battle of the Nile.

The church stands almost alone, surrounded by open fields. The Rev Nelson came here in 1755 with his young wife Catherine,

Nelson's birthplace, the Old Rectory at Burnham Thorpe

and they are buried under the floor of the chancel. Outside are the graves of Horatio's brother Maurice and sister Susannah. There's a fine memorial to the naval hero himself, incorporating a lifelike bust, on the chancel wall and beside this are further memorials to his parents. At the back of the church are copies of two important documents, the certificate of his baptism and a copy of entries in the church register in relation to a wedding where one of the witnesses was Horatio, then almost eleven years old.

There are also a number of relics from HMS *Victory*, the main one being a large wooden cross mounted on the rood beam across the chancel arch. It is made from the ship's original timbers, as is the wooden lectern below. On the wall at the entrance to the base of the bell tower is a wood and copper tablet commemorating restoration of the church bell in 1958. Again, materials in this plaque come from the *Victory*.

A statue of Nelson stands in the ground of Norwich Cathedral, near the school he attended. His monument on the South Denes at Great Yarmouth was completed in 1819, the tall column intended to act as a seamark to assist ships in the navigation along the Norfolk coast. Built of white stone, it stands 144 ft high with the figure of Britannia on top, facing inland.

The most common form of Nelson memorial results from the tradition of naming pubs after famous people and events, and we find the Lord Nelson, the Norfolk Hero or simply the Hero. Ironically, the Lord Nelson at Burnham Thorpe, his home patch, was originally called the Plough and didn't adopt its present name until 1807. There's an amusing yarn told of the Wrestler's Inn at Yarmouth where Nelson stayed when he reached England in 1800 after travelling overland from Italy, and again after the Battle of Copenhagen. Informed of a plan to rename the inn the Nelson Arms in his honour, he is said to have quipped: 'That would be absurd, seeing as I have only one arm!'

Happily, Norfolk's most famous son is mainly celebrated with quiet pride rather than crass commercialism. Burnham Thorpe, I suspect, hasn't changed that much since he lived and played here as a boy. The river runs through the centre of the village and it's easy to imagine a young lad following its course until he came to the tidal estuary at Burnham Overy Staithe. Here he would have caught his first glimpse of the sea that was to be his destiny. Perhaps he chatted to local fishermen about winds and tides and recalled their words of wisdom as his epic career unfolded.

On a cold, wet January day in 1806, London saw the largest state funeral procession ever staged in the capital. Tens of thousands silently lined the route from Whitehall to St Paul's Cathedral and a great naval victory was nearly overshadowed by the death of its architect. The entire nation was in mourning for a hero from Norfolk.

19

Thomas Paine (1737–1809)

Author of The Rights of Man

While innovators in the late 18th century normally relied on social position or friends in high places to make their case, Thomas Paine was hounded by the rulers of his own country as a dangerous subversive; but he was revered as a prophet in France and the future United States of America. In fact, no political writer made a more immediate impact on his own time than Norfolk-born Paine.

His success and enduring reputation were founded largely on his brilliance as a phrasemaker. His pamphlet *Common Sense* crystallised the arguments for independence that fuelled the American Revolution. His *The Rights of Man*, penned in defence of the French Revolution, made him the spokesman for English radicalism against the oppressive traditions of the 18th century. It sold 200,000 copies and caused Paine to be tried for seditious libel and his effigy to be hung, shot and burned. His *Age of Reason* was the first book to come out and say in plain English that the Bible was irrational and inconsistent, and that it was not the voice of God. He dealt with the big issues and took it for granted they were everybody's to consider.

Paine could also compose such rousing trumpet-calls as 'These are the times that try men's souls,' 'The sublime and the ridiculous are often so nearly related that it is difficult to class them separately,' 'He pities the plumage, but forgets the dying bird,' and 'My country is the world and my religion is to do good.' Nearly two centuries after his death these phrases still command the rich heights of radical rhetoric.

THOMAS PAINE (1737–1809)

Thomas Paine

The roots of Paine's political passion were in his father's Quakerism, and sermons in the Thetford meeting house gave him a grounding in pacifism and a belief that humanitarianism could be an end in itself. Paine's father also ran a small farm and so made enough money to send the boy to the local grammar school from the age of 6 until he was 14. Apprenticed to his father, he too became a corset-maker, later moving to Sandwich to open a shop selling 'ladies' foundation garments'. He married the daughter of an exciseman and took up the more manly occupation of the customs service.

Soon widowed, Paine moved to Lewes in Sussex where he joined the underground world of radical politics and became a member of the splendidly-named Headstrong Club to argue about the righting of social wrongs. It was there he met Benjamin Franklin, the American political journalist and scientist who gave him a letter of introduction – effectively a passport to America. As he set sail in 1774, these were Franklin's words of endorsement: 'An ingenious, worthy young man.' As his stock rose as an energetic and influential political journalist, Paine published *Common Sense* in 1776 advocating complete independence from the British Crown.

He returned to England in 1787 and three years later his book *The Rights of Man* poured scorn on the British constitution: 'To inherit a Government is to inherit the People, as if they were flocks and herds.' The book, described by radical historian E.P. Thompson as 'the foundation text of the English working-class movement', was regarded as seditious in the climate of fear gripping Britain as the French Revolution lurched from radical reform to bloody class warfare.

Paine fled to France after being charged with treason. He was welcomed as a hero of social revolution at first and elected to the National Convention, but was distrusted by Robespierre and put in prison. While himself under the shadow of the guillotine during the Reign of Terror of 1794, Paine worked on *The Age of Reason*. He was released a year after his arrest when Robespierre was overthrown and executed.

The rise from corset-maker to hero of revolutions in two foreign nations, and hero or villain in his own, was a remarkable achievement. Paine was much more than an agitator, putting forward theories that would be embraced by any 20th century socialist. He called for the cutting of government costs and defence expenditure and the introduction of income tax, which would rise to 100 per cent at an annual income of £23,000.

Money raised would fund education for all children, marriage, maternity and family allowances, financial and housing aid for the unemployed and old age pensions.

Paine's international career had a sad ending. Returning to what was now the United States of America in 1802, he found his contribution to the birth of a nation largely forgotten. He died seven years later in poverty in New York. In 1819 William Cobbett brought his remains home to England but their whereabouts are no longer known. Paine had to wait until 1945 to be elected to the American Hall of Fame and so stand alongside George Washington and Paul Revere.

Before a statue of Paine was erected in his home town of Thetford in 1964 there had been only a bronze plaque paid for by American airmen stationed in the area during the Second World War. The gilded bronze figure – sculpted by Sir Charles

The statue of Thomas Paine at Thetford

Wheeler, at one time President of the Royal Academy – stands on an inscribed stone base, a muscular Paine in period dress, clutching a copy of *The Rights of Man* and pointing a quill pen towards America. The Thetford authorities were urged to accept the gift by the Tom Paine Foundation of New York, and it is one of just a few statues in England raised by foreign request.

The political dispute over the statue led to the founding of the Thomas Paine Society of which former Labour leader Michael Foot became president. While the 200th anniversary of Paine's birth had been marked by little more than a dinner in the Guildhall in London, the Society saw to it that the 250th anniversary in 1987 was widely acclaimed.

In his biography of Paine, published in 1988, Professor A.J. Ayer concluded: 'He thought that all men without exception should have as large a say as was practically possible in the management of their own affairs, and he combined this with a recognition of the need for society to take responsibility for those of its members who were not in a position to fend adequately for themselves. Consequently, he repudiated unearned privilege. He was willing that men should battle for their rights, but assumed that once they had obtained them they would be bound to perceive the futility of war.'

20

Lucilla Reeve (1889–1950)

The Breckland Rebel

Lucilla Reeve was born out of wedlock and was killed by her own hand, so she may seem an unlikely choice as a Norfolk heroine. For all that, her taking on of Breckland's unforgiving soil and wartime military might in the Stanford Battle Area is a truly compelling story – still waiting to be fully acknowledged.

It was in the autumn of 1950 that this short, stocky figure dressed in country tweeds walked into the half-light of a chicken-plucking shed that was her makeshift home. A few hours later her body was found hanging from a beam. It was an ignominious end for the woman who had risen from impoverished roots to become the land agent at a top Norfolk estate and then wrought miracles on a derelict farm when the government annexed five villages for military use. She became a defiant refugee on her own land.

Lucilla was the illegitimate daughter of a parlourmaid and the identity of her father remains a mystery. Her mother Polly worked for the influential Walsingham family whose grand shooting parties on the Merton Estate near Watton included members of the Royal Family. A secret benefactor paid for Lucilla's private education in London. Her rise to the position of Land Agent on the estate was remarkable in a class conscious era.

A devout Christian, Lucilla had visions, believed in ghosts and could divine water. By the 1930s she was in charge of the day-to-day running of the 14,000 acre estate, but she raised eyebrows by cutting her hair short and dressing like a man. Hilda Perry, who lived on the estate, recalled: 'She was way ahead of her time. She was really clever and you had to admire her. She knew everything and everybody. She went tearing around in a little red sports car, and people called her Miss Madcap.'

But Lucilla was interested in politics and they called her less flattering names when, like many other well-connected people of the time, she flirted with Oswald Mosley's Blackshirts. She even had her photograph taken standing next to the National Socialist leader. She had been a staunch Conservative since 1922 and was a Tory platform speaker during the 1931 election campaign. She had served on the local area guardians' committee and the Wayland Rural District Council, becoming vice-chairman of the rating and valuation committee.

Her interest in the British Union of Fascists dated from May 1935, when she attended Mosley's meeting at Swaffham with the intention of heckling. But she was so impressed by what he said that she abandoned her Conservative affiliations and immediately signed up as an active member. She told the *Eastern Daily Press*: 'I did not know much about politics then and I don't know much about them now. And I don't suppose that I ever shall; that's why I am standing for Parliament.'

She failed to gain any kind of significant following. With the outbreak of war in 1939, Lucilla's views made her an increasingly controversial character. She was tolerated, even respected, on the Merton Estate, although some small boys made mock Nazi salutes behind her back. But her presence concerned officials and public reaction to the Dunkirk evacuation fuelled rumours that the BUF's parliamentary candidate for South-West Norfolk was a Nazi agent. She was taken into custody by the military but released 'after the usual search and interrogation'.

The present Lord Walsingham remembers: 'They wanted to intern her. My father had already been called up as an "old but bold" and naturally he didn't want to lose his highly capable land agent. So he offered to shoot her if the Germans landed and on that basis she stayed here. I don't think she ever knew my father was obliged to kill her if they invaded.'

Just prior to the outbreak of war, in 1938, eight farms owned by the estate had had to be let. Lucilla found tenants for seven but she decided to take the other one herself. Typically, she created order out of chaos, rearing pigs, sheep, cattle, goats and ducks as well as cultivating crops and finding time to plant thousands of trees. Then a bombshell came on 13th June 1942: her farm was wanted for military purposes. Everybody in that group of Breckland villages of Stanford, Tottington, Stuston, Langford and Buckenham Tofts was given notice to quit with a promise they would be able to return after the war – a promise that was never to be fulfilled.

A stubborn Lucilla simply refused to move. She continued to live in her home at Bagmore, but eventually the sight and sound

Lucilla Reeve in amongst the sheep

of tanks churning up her fields and knocking down barns and outbuildings proved too much. She acquired three wooden chicken huts and a tin garage and set them just outside the northern boundary of the Battle Area. Defiant, she waited for the chance to return. However, as the years passed she felt the effect of all the strains. She was devastated to see her erstwhile home transformed into a ghost village and wrote of 'the ruin and desolation of a village I'd only seven years ago described as lovely.' She referred to 'the dead and staring eyes of the cottage windows, the ruins of what had once been my home.'

Realisation that the government would not return the land to its inhabitants proved the crushing blow for Lucilla, and so it was that a man venturing into Merton Woods found her body in the autumn of 1950. She had been suffering from fits of depression, hallucinations and illusions. The inquest found she had committed suicide while she was disturbed. Local villagers were certain that it was the loss of her farm and livelihood in the war that led her to take her own life.

There's no headstone in Tottington church to mark the passing of this eccentric character. However, visitors cannot fail to notice the strange bulge at one corner of the churchyard. Lucilla was buried outside consecrated ground because she had committed suicide. Ironically, when the Ministry of Defence put up a fence, they brought Lucilla Reeve's grave into the churchyard and so unwittingly reunited her with the community about which she cared so passionately.

Sadly, her diaries, letters and private papers have not survived, but she wrote regular articles for the *Eastern Daily Press* and the *Farmer's Weekly*. Many of these were collected together in her books. *The Pheasants Had No Tails* contains short stories and poetry – she sent patriotic verses to the Royal Family on special occasions – while *The Earth No Longer Bare* and *Farming On a Battle Ground* tell of her farming experiences.

Tanks in the battle area where Lucilla Reeve took on the military

So is she a Norfolk heroine? She was certainly a doughty fighter who dug deep into Breckland's past for the roots of physical endurance and mental tenacity, and she is beginning to be seen as a leading symbol of resistance to Norfolk's biggest and most traumatic land-grab of the 20th century. Yes, she did go out of her way to attract criticism, not least in the political arena at a sensitive time. But she defied many odds and prejudices to plough her own highly individual furrow. It would have been so easy for her to have settled for more comfortable pastures among the local gentry.

21

Derek Seagrim (1903–1943) and Hugh Seagrim (1909–1944)

The Wartime Valour of Two Norfolk Brothers

The only brothers ever to win the country's top two awards for bravery shared a common Norfolk heritage and an altogether uncommon brand of valour.

Derek and Hugh Seagrim were raised in the village of Whissonsett, a few miles from Fakenham, and both attended the King Edward VI School standing in the shadow of Norwich Cathedral. Both made their careers in the Army and both were destined to die on foreign fields in the Second World War, displaying the kind of self-sacrifice that was to earn them a unique posthumous distinction. While Derek's valour was recognised by the award of the Victoria Cross, his younger brother's dauntless heroism was marked with a George Cross. Their mother Annabel went to Buckingham Palace to receive both awards from King George VI.

Derek and Hugh were among five sons born to the Rev Charles Seagrim, the Rector of Whissonsett-with-Horningtoft. They all were to become professional soldiers – the eldest, Charles, in the Royal Artillery, Cyril in the Royal Engineers, Derek in the Green Howards and Jack and Hugh in the Indian Army.

The Rev Seagrim, a former missionary in South Africa, had arrived in rural Norfolk on a pony and trap in 1909 and settled into the village rectory with its eight bedrooms, sprawling gardens and menagerie of pets. 'We were as poor as church mice,' Jack later recalled. 'We had our own cows, goats and pigs. We even had to pump our own water from a well in the yard. But

Hugh and Derek Seagrim

for all that it was an immensely happy childhood.'

Although he did not shine academically, Derek proved an accomplished cricketer, turning out for village and school teams, and also displaying talent for middle-distance running. Hugh shared his elder brother's sporting prowess. He excelled at football where his height – he was 6 ft 4 in tall – made him an effective goalkeeper. Their army careers were marked by steady if unremarkable progress until the outbreak of war. Soldiering in different parts of the world meant they met only rarely. Derek spent the early part of the war as a staff officer responsible for air liaison in East Africa and Greece. As a result of heavy losses during fighting around Tobruk in 1942, he was given his first command, the 7th Green Howards.

Charged with reconstructing the shattered unit in readiness for the Alamein offensive, he made an immediate impact. A slim and wiry figure, he soon won the devotion of his men and his outstanding leadership reached a climax during the assault on the

Mareth Line in March 1943. A natural defensive barrier of immense strength, the fortifications were covered by a formidable anti-tank ditch. The leading wave, carrying scaling ladders, doubled forward straight into a hail of bullets. A few scrambled into the ditch and the attack stalled in the face of withering fire. Derek Seagrim marched into the open and waved on the disorganised troops like a policeman on traffic duty. Then his blood was up. He climbed one of the scaling ladders and attacked the massed machine guns with revolver and grenades. He killed or captured 20 of the defenders. Inspired by his astonishing courage, the tattered remnants of the assault companies blasted and bombed their way into the seemingly impregnable fortress. Amid the tornado of fire, Seagrim was seen calmly walking along the top of the anti-tank ditch directing operations.

Two months after a remarkable victory against all odds, the *London Gazette* announced the award of the Victoria Cross to Lt Col Derek Antony Seagrim. The citation praised his utter disregard for personal safety and concluded: 'He so inspired his men that the battalion took and held its objective, thereby allowing the attack to proceed.' Tragically, he did not live to read those words. He died of his wounds 16 days after the Mareth battle.

While Derek was leading his men with such distinction in North Africa, his brother Hugh was engaged in an altogether more unconventional campaign, thousands of miles further east in the jungle-clad Karen hills of Burma. Having volunteered to stay behind when the British retreated to the borders of India, he organised resistance against the Japanese army of occupation. Adopting native dress, he lived among the Karen tribesmen by whom he was known, on account of his size, as 'Grandfather Longlegs'.

His guerrilla forces provided vital intelligence which he was able to pass on to India. Such was his skill and quiet daring that the authorities awarded him a DSO and made him an MBE. More British officers were parachuted into the hills, but as Hugh Seagrim's clandestine operations grew so did the Japanese effort to destroy his secret network. Helped by loyal villagers, he narrowly avoided capture many times. Two fellow officers were ambushed and killed and the Japanese sent word to Seagrim that more tribesmen would be executed if he didn't give himself up. Despite the pleadings of his Karen guerrillas, he agreed to surrender in an attempt to avert further bloodshed – but in the full knowledge that he was signing his own death warrant.

The village sign at Whissonsett with the Seagrim brothers as centrepiece

Six months later, after a military trial, 'Grandfather Longlegs' was driven out of Rangoon Jail to face his execution. His thin, emaciated body was scarred with scabies but he is said to have still managed a final defiant smile.

To the end he had pleaded with the Japanese to spare the Karens any further suffering. 'I do not mind what you do to me,' he declared, 'but I do ask you . . . punish only me.' After the full story of his stirring self-sacrifice became known, he was posthumously awarded the George Cross.

The brothers' bravery earned fresh tributes on a summer afternoon in 1985 when the people of Whissonsett gathered for the unveiling of a new village sign, displaying as its centrepiece the carved twin figures of Derek and Hugh Seagrim. Corporal Ray Pagani, who served with Major Hugh in Burma, was close to tears as he recalled: 'He was a deeply religious man who carried a Bible in one hand and a tommy-gun in the other. He gave himself up so the tribesmen might live.'

There was more praise for the pair from Lt Col Don Stow of the Green Howards and from the sole surviving brother, Lt Col Jack Seagrim, who said the new sign should honour all villagers who died in the war.

22

Allan Smethurst (1927–2000)

The Singing Postman

The shy, buck-toothed and bespectacled figure in a postman's uniform hardly cut a dash on or off stage. For many he was no more than a passing rustic novelty act soaked in homely nostalgia. And yet, remarkably, Allan Smethurst has come to symbolise Norfolk's proud independent streak; eccentric, perhaps, but worthy of prolonged applause in an increasingly standardised world.

The Singing Postman even outsold the Beatles and Rolling Stones for a time when his catchy anthem *Hev Yew Gotta Loight, Boy?* raced into the national pop charts in 1965. He scaled such television heights as *Top of the Pops*, *Sunday Night at the London Palladium* and the *Des O'Connor Show*. He was signed up for a bill-topping summer season on Great Yarmouth's Golden Mile. He opened fêtes and shops and was mobbed by fans outside the Co-op in Stowmarket. He starred in a colour film made to promote him in the USA. He didn't cross the Atlantic, and the film was never shown in public, but the fact it was put together with the American market in mind reminds us just how big an impact he made when an unlikely career took off.

Allan Smethurst took the Norfolk accent to places it had never been before. The simple, plaintive delivery of his lyrics sat easily with the predictable strum of his guitar as he sang of a place he loved and lamented. Despite obvious personal frailties that were bound to cut short his spell in the limelight, he adopted his own highly individual stance in the glorious but vain battle to hold back the tide of change. He wanted Norfolk to stay in a gentle

Allan Smethurst, the singing postman

childhood groove while the rest of the planet kept on spinning itself daft and dizzy. He did suggest *Yew Carnt Keep Livin' In The Parst*, but even as he wrote and warbled we sensed every note was loaded with regret.

He couldn't halt 'progress', but he could point with genuine concern to what it was replacing. Audiences identified closely with that dilemma, especially in a fast-changing countryside, and still nod sympathetically as his lyrics continue to emphasise qualities blatantly surrendered to urban tentacles. The Singing Postman was a 'green' performer long before environmental issues became fashionable.

Allan was born in Bury, Lancashire, but he moved to Sheringham on the North Norfolk coast as a two year old and fond childhood memories inspired many of his songs. Indeed, his writing flair sprang from far deeper wells than any desire or ability to perform on stage. Winsome, wistful and witty compositions deserve to be shared as slices of social history wrapped in the endearing delights of the Norfolk dialect. Allan worried that he would be remembered for just one number, *Hev Yew Gotta Loight, Boy?*, but there are many other notable songs, deceptively simple but crammed with potent images of a Norfolk life fast disappearing even as he wrote and sang about it.

It may be a mite fanciful to call him East Anglia's Robbie Burns, but Allan's lyrics stand in their own right as potent signposts to a cherished past – the hiss of steam on the old railway line; following the binder round; the old-style community pub where they still play dommies in the bar; and the village cricket match where the poacher is caught out for a duck and the dentist pulls out the stumps.

Possibly his soft melancholy nature, clearly at odds with the cynical and savage show business world, made it inevitable that the round as a national celebrity would end sooner rather than later. Illness brought on by stage fright and excessive drinking cut short time in the spotlight for a £12-a-week postman who moved into the big league and during his singing career earned over £20,000. But when he signed on the dole in 1970 he candidly admitted: 'I've been foolish and spent the lot.' He lived much of the rest of his life as a virtual recluse in a Salvation Army hostel in Grimsby, continuing to write songs even when he could no longer play the guitar because of arthritis. Shortly before he died in December 2000 he was visited by entertainer Rolf Harris, who led the parade of Singing Postman imitators with distinction.

A widespread re-awakening of interest in Allan's work in recent years has seen a new generation tune into songs given the modern CD treatment, a series to underline just how much good material did flow from his pen. The East Anglian Film Archive produced a video about him – including that colour film made to promote him in the USA – and I compiled a book on his life and lyrics. Special evenings are held in Norfolk and Suffolk to celebrate his birthday on 18th November, with enthusiasts pulling on a postman's uniform before bursting into tribute renditions. *Hev Yew Gotta Loight, Boy?* still casts a potent spell, not least among exiles way beyond Norfolk's boundaries.

Allan Smethurst's enduring appeal is based on acceptance that homely but vulnerable characters can be far more interesting than those with inflated egos and paper-thin talents. His songs are rooted in time and place but retain charm and value because they are unpretentious, gently amusing, generally accessible and admirably self-effacing. Those who criticised him at the time when fame called for yokel stereotypes of Norfolk people, may now realise he was motivated much more by local pride and passion than any need for adulation or demands for gimmicks.

An unlikely standard bearer for the county and it's 'dew diffrunt' mantra, he'd probably feel wholly embarrassed at being included on any Norfolk roll of honour. I place him there unreservedly because he found enough courage to defy all the odds and take on personal demons long enough to transport his gentler, slower and kinder world into forbidding territory. Results of a colourful if all-too-brief mission linger on in the lasting familiarity, constant freshness and genuine affection surrounding the Singing Postman's compositions.

23

Doreen Wallace (1897–1989)

Campaigner Against The Tithe

She claimed William Wallace as an ancestor. Although not directly descended from him, Doreen Wallace certainly came from the same extensive family network as the great Scottish patriot who led resistance against Edward I, was captured, condemned for treason and executed in 1305 and whose exploits inspired a successful recent film.

As a social campaigner and writer, Doreen gained widespread recognition as the key figure in a 40 year campaign to abolish what she described as 'the iniquitous tithe tax.' On her death at 92, the *Eastern Daily Press* called her 'a latter-day Boadicea. Here was no ordinary lady of the manor. She remained a trenchant East Anglian non-conformist of the secular kind almost up to the end of her life.'

The compulsory tithe originated from medieval times as a form of tribute consisting of a tenth of a man's property and produce, connected politically with taxation and in religious terms with the offering of first fruits to the deity. While there is no proof that the tithe was ever intended to be a tax purely on agriculture, for 100,000 English and Welsh farmers such was the reality at the start of the 20th century. And with the farming crash in the years immediately following the end of the First World War the tithe system brought ruin to thousands of small farming families ensnared in economic depression.

Resulting protests, demonstrations and direct action by many of those 100,000 farmers, as well as by landowners and supporters, was one of the most remarkable social and political

Doreen Wallace held aloft by supporters in her fight against the tithe tax

agitations of the restless inter-war years. The anti-tithe movement took on the Establishment long before it was either easy or fashionable. It was a war in which Norfolk, Suffolk and Essex, the most heavily-tithed counties, were chief battlegrounds. It became a war of arrests, evictions, enforced auctions and bankruptcies. In Norfolk and Suffolk two of the leaders in the anti-tithe movement were farmer's wife and teacher Doreen Wallace of Wortham, near Diss, and farmer Albert Mobbs of Oulton Broad, near Lowestoft.

Doreen Wallace became the last president of the National Tithe Payers' Association in 1939. Four years earlier she and her husband Roland barricaded their farm during a six-week siege after her refusal to pay the Church of England tithe. Eventually 134 pigs and 15 cattle worth £700 were seized in lieu of the tax, and a memorial recording the event was erected. In the summer of 1939 she decided to see if the church really would make a person bankrupt – so she refused to pay again. This time her furniture and bedding were taken from the home and auctioned. However, the auctioneer was a good friend and the furniture was bought by other members of the Association. By nightfall it was all back in Wortham Manor.

With the arrival of war, the tithe controversy was effectively finished as a political issue. By the late 1940s, with price guarantees and financial inducements taking British agriculture into a new and prosperous era, many farmers redeemed their tithes. In fact, tithing became an Inland Revenue issue with final payments scheduled for 1996. But by 1977 it had become so expensive to collect that the Government called it a day.

A few months before her death in 1989, Doreen Wallace was writing letters railing against the way farming was going within the EEC and also leading a revolt of Diss residents, organising a protest group against the local council who wanted to change the number of her home and those of her neighbours. The council backed down.

Doreen had moved to Norfolk to take up a teaching post in Diss after the First World War. Over the years she wrote nearly 50 novels as well as short stories, poems and several works of non-fiction. Like Dorothy Sayers, who was a contemporary at Oxford, she became known as one of the Somerville College novelists. In 1931 she published her first, *A Little Learning*, which clearly foreshadowed the two central concerns that were to guide her writing and her life – education and farming. In East Anglia she had observed that there was 'something odd about land – it possesses the possessors, it grapples them to its soul with hooks of steel.'

Her best work features observant accounts of personal and social relations in village life, farming and school, all with a sharp eye for idiom. 'Her books are all her own, and I like them very much,' said Sir John Betjeman. Sadly, they are out of print and we wait for an overdue revival of interest in a highly-aware social commentator, a chronicler of life in country towns and villages, not unlike Mrs Gaskell of the northern communities.

In 1951 Doreen teamed up with naturalist Dick Bagnall-Oakeley to produce the Norfolk volume in the popular County Books series. She wrote in a typically forthright manner about her adopted home: 'It is a fact that after a "foreigner" has lived twenty years in the county he is still a new arrival; he may, however, be accepted by that time as the kind of new arrival who will be made welcome if he cares to settle down . . . Norfolk is not on the way to anywhere. Trains going to Norfolk go no further, for there is only the sea beyond. Travellers only come into the county because they have family or business connections there, that is to say, they are either Norfolk people or thoroughly used to Norfolk ways . . . In addition, there is a formidable dialect, oddly pronounced and highly idiomatic; this makes strangers, in their inability to cope with it, both feel and look doubly strange.'

Well over 30 years later, in an article for the *Eastern Daily Press*, Doreen sized up the growing colonisation of some parts of the county: 'There are people in villages who have never spoken together, who are not known to the real villagers either by sight or by name . . . the most useless "foreigners" are those whose country retreat is only meant for weekend and summer breaks. They don't even arrive unless the weather invites. They can never become part of country life.'

Doreen Wallace battled long and hard to help win the tithe war. She wrote prolifically for 60 years, casting a learned but honest eye over a landscape and people she came to appreciate and understand. 'A rum lot – but worth the effort!' was her uplifting verdict.

24

James Woodforde (1740–1803)

Parson and Celebrated Diarist

Much of what we know about daily life in Norfolk during the second half of the 18th century is down to a sociable parson who kept a diary from the age of 18 until a few weeks before his death – a span of well over 40 years. Born in Somerset and educated at New College, Oxford, James Woodforde held a number of curacies before being appointed in 1774 to the living of Weston Longville, a few miles north-west of Norwich. First published in the 1920s, the five-volume diary places him alongside Kilvert, Evelyn and Pepys as a chronicler of his time.

As a result of his style, particularly the relish with which he described enormous meals, Woodforde has long been ripe for parody. Yet he demonstrated the value of the educated parson to village life in binding the social structure with the cement of his learning, preaching and good works.

While his diary is a mine of information about the lives of ordinary people – farmers, shopkeepers, servants, squires, clergy, doctors, blacksmiths and merchants – Woodforde also provides sharp pictures of outstanding historical events as they were seen at the time. For example, on 29th November 1798, he noted: 'Great Rejoicings at Norwich today as Lord Nelson's late great and noble Victory over the French near Alexandria in Egypt. An Ox roasted whole in the Market-Place. This being a day of general Thanksgiving Mr Cotman read Prayers this morning at Weston Church, proper on the occasion.'

The coming of aeronautics was reported like this on 1st June

1765: 'About 3 o'clock this Afternoon a violent Tempest arose at Norwich . . . very loud thunder and strong white Lightening with heavy Rain . . . immediately after which Mr Decker's Balloon with Decker himself in a boat attached to it ascended from Quantrell's Gardens and very majestically. It was out of sight in about 10 minutes . . . I saw it from Brecondale Hill and it went almost over my Head . . .'

A gentle stroll round the good parson's patch today as it strains to maintain a toehold on the countryside near Norwich hardly qualifies as a tour of celebration. Traffic thunders through to drown birdsong, and there's part of the Bernard Matthews turkey empire on the old aerodrome. On the other side of the village is a Dinosaur Park tourist attraction. Even so, the still, small voice of thanksgiving can yet be heard by seeking refuge in the splendidly spacious All Saints' church, the welcoming Parson Woodforde pub opposite and a clutch of attractive houses vying for a place on a calendar extolling the delights of rural retirement.

Woodforde clearly appreciated the comparative comfort in which he lived on about £400 a year and showed regular charity towards itinerants who called at the rectory. He didn't ask for fees for marriages or burials and when local farmers brought him their annual tithe, it descended rapidly into a 'frolic', full of beer and bonhomie. Such a generous nature is enshrined in the memorial tablet on the chancel wall in Weston Longville church, just above a diamond-shaped tile indicating his burial place. The tablet was erected by his nephew Bill and faithful niece Nancy, who looked after him for so many years: 'His parishioners held him in the highest esteem and veneration and as a tribute to his memory followed him to the grave. The poor feel a severe loss as they were the constant objects of his bounty.'

Woodforde referred to his musings as a 'trifling' book and could have nursed no ambitions to see it emerge as one of the most telling summaries of the Georgian age. This work of an ordinary

James Woodforde

man is now accepted as extraordinary for the insight it gives to domestic and social life in the last four decades of the 18th century. Just as significantly, it is highly entertaining. Noisy toads, drunken pigs, pregnant maids, nuisance woodpeckers, strange dreams, November primroses, June tempests, cruel winters and countless other topics seek our attention.

Although Parson Woodforde never married, he did propose to a Miss Betsy White of Shepton Mallet in 1774. She jilted him later for a rich man from Devonshire. Our Norfolk Bachelor of Divinity was not averse to a spot of flirting, and he recounts taking off a young widow's garter and good-naturedly exchanging a pair of his garters for a pair of hers!

It is this spirited, almost earthy, side of his character that endears him to so many through pages sparkling now as brightly as the waters of the Wensum where he landed pike and trout over two centuries ago. He resided in his living, looking after parishioners himself instead of making do with an underpaid curate. He bought gin and cognac from smugglers, lapped up good food washed down with port and Madeira and gambled regularly at cards, albeit for small stakes. An impish sense of humour shines through many incidents recorded in the diary, not least New Year celebrations: 'Nancy and Betsie Davie locked me in the great parlour, and both fell on me and pulled my wig almost to pieces – I paid them for it, however.'

He says so much about meals that a reputation for gluttony has grown over the years. Even so, some enthusiasts claim he should be indicted merely for conviviality. He loved good company, and food simply paved the way for some intimacy and pleasure in what was a rather lonely existence. It's also worth noting the old custom of cramming the table with many dishes of roast, game and fish instead of serving them as separate courses. Woodforde extended the pleasures involved by including the day's menus in his diary – even in the final words written in October 1802: 'Very weak this Morning, scarce able to put on my Clothes and with great difficulty, get down Stairs with help . . . Dinner to day, Roast Beef etc.' He died on New Year's Day 1803.

So, a Norfolk diary of the commonplace has become part of our rich inheritance. Parson Woodforde serves as an inspiration to all who vow to keep daily records, and then find an exciting challenge turning into a tedious chore before January has burst into double figures!

Index

A Mind to Murder

P. D. James (1920–2014) was born in Oxford and educated at Cambridge High School for Girls. From 1949 to 1968 she worked in the National Health Service and subsequently the Home Office, first in the Police Department and later in the Criminal Policy Department. All that experience was used in her novels. She was a Fellow of the Royal Society of Literature and of the Royal Society of Arts and served as a Governor of the BBC, a member of the Arts Council, where she was Chairman of the Literary Advisory Panel, on the Board of the British Council and as a magistrate in Middlesex and London. She was an Honorary Bencher of the Honourable Society of the Inner Temple. She won awards for crime writing in Britain, America, Italy and Scandinavia, including the Mystery Writers of America Grandmaster Award and the National Arts Club Medal of Honor for Literature (US). She received honorary degrees from seven British universities, was awarded an OBE in 1983 and was created a life peer in 1991. In 1997 she was elected President of the Society of Authors, stepping down from the post in August 2013.

by the same author

COVER HER FACE
UNNATURAL CAUSES
SHROUD FOR A NIGHTINGALE
AN UNSUITABLE JOB FOR A WOMAN
THE BLACK TOWER
DEATH OF AN EXPERT WITNESS
INNOCENT BLOOD
THE SKULL BENEATH THE SKIN
A TASTE FOR DEATH
DEVICES AND DESIRES
THE CHILDREN OF MEN
ORIGINAL SIN
A CERTAIN JUSTICE
DEATH IN HOLY ORDERS
THE MURDER ROOM
THE LIGHTHOUSE
THE PRIVATE PATIENT
DEATH COMES TO PEMBERLEY
THE MISTLETOE MURDER AND OTHER STORIES
SLEEP NO MORE: SIX MURDEROUS TALES

non-fiction

TIME TO BE IN EARNEST
A fragment of Autobiography

THE MAUL AND THE PEAR TREE
The Ratcliffe Highway Murders 1811
(by P. D. James and T. A. Critchley)

TALKING ABOUT DETECTIVE FICTION